KINGDOM
POLITICS

TONY
EVANS

MOODY PUBLISHERS
CHICAGO

Portions of the Introduction are excerpted from *How Should Christians Vote*, © 2012 by Anthony T. Evans. Portions of chapter 8 are excerpted from *The Kingdom Agenda: Life Under God*, © 2000 by Anthony T. Evans.

Scripture quotations, unless otherwise indicated, are taken from the New American Standard Bible®, Copyright © 1960, 1962, 1963, 1968, 1971, 1972, 1973, 1975, 1977, 1995 by The Lockman Foundation. Used by permission. www.Lockman.org

Edited by Kevin Mungons
Interior design: Ragont Design
Cover design: Greg Jackson and Erik M. Peterson
Cover illustration of continental USA © 2021 by Warisara Pearprai/iStock (1343489387). All rights reserved.
Author photo credit: Tayte Rian Gerik

Library of Congress Cataloging-in-Publication Data

Names: Evans, Tony, 1949- author.
Title: Kingdom politics : returning God to government / Dr. Tony Evans.
Description: Chicago : Moody Publishers, [2022] | Includes bibliographical
   references and index. | Summary: "Christians love to talk about
   politics, but the current conversation is full of contentious words that
   divide our churches and families. Dr. Tony Evans takes a step back to
   find foundational Bible principles for integrating politics into our
   daily lives. Kingdom Politics offers a biblical path through one of the
   most divisive issues of our time"-- Provided by publisher.
Identifiers: LCCN 2022007917 (print) | LCCN 2022007918 (ebook) | ISBN
   9780802428981 (paperback) | ISBN 9780802474193 (ebook)
Subjects: LCSH: Christianity and politics. | BISAC: RELIGION / Christian
   Living / Social Issues
Classification: LCC BR115.P7 E935 2022 (print) | LCC BR115.P7 (ebook) |
   DDC 261.7--dc23/eng/20220308
LC record available at https://lccn.loc.gov/2022007917
LC ebook record available at https://lccn.loc.gov/2022007918

Originally delivered by fleets of horse-drawn wagons, the affordable paperbacks from D. L. Moody's publishing house resourced the church and served everyday people. Now, after more than 125 years of publishing and ministry, Moody Publishers' mission remains the same—even if our delivery systems have changed a bit. For more information on other books (and resources) created from a biblical perspective, go to www.moodypublishers.com or write to:

Moody Publishers
820 N. LaSalle Boulevard
Chicago, IL 60610

1 3 5 7 9 10 8 6 4 2

Printed in the United States of America

CONTENTS

Introduction

POLITICS AND THE KINGDOM AGENDA

Y ou cannot read the Bible and ignore the political realm. The Bible is thick with politics. You have four books (1 and 2 Kings and 1 and 2 Chronicles) that deal with the rule and reign of government leaders. Scripture is packed with political concerns including laws, statutes, ordinances, kingdoms, empires, courts, judges, kings, queens, taxes, and so much more.

God is active on virtually every page engaging in the political affairs of humanity for both blessing and judgment. You might say that the Bible is a political textbook since God is seen setting up nations, writing constitutions and by-laws. He both establishes governments and dismantles them. He places people in strategic political roles and removes others from their political perches.

Given this reality, it is unfortunate that God and politics are far too often disconnected from each other as though connecting them too closely is anathema. The failure to properly connect God's relationship to politics based on His Word has left individuals, political leaders, and nations void of the knowledge needed to govern society as the Creator intended.

If you were to come to me with your personal life in shambles and you didn't know which way to turn, and you said, "Tony Evans, help me," I would open up my Bible, identify the cause of your personal dilemma, and speak God's truth about your situation—giving you God's resolution for whatever it is that you are facing and then ask the Holy Spirit to empower your ability to respond in obedience to God's Word.

If you were to come to me with your family life in shambles with both you and your spouse seeking a divorce because of chaos in your home, and you said, "Tony Evans, help me," again I would open up my Bible, identify the cause of your familial dilemma, and present to you God's solution for whatever it is that you are facing and then ask the Holy Spirit to empower your ability to respond in obedience to God's Word.

If you were a pastor of a church and you came to me with your deacons or elder board because your church was in shambles, everyone was arguing, and your congregation was confused, and you said, "Tony Evans, help us," I would open the very same Bible that I used to help the individual and the family, and I would identify the cause for the chaos based on the Word of God, seeking to prescribe biblical solutions for the calamity in your church and then ask the Holy Spirit to empower your ability to respond in obedience to God's Word.

In other words, Scripture would not only solve the individual and family divisions, but it would also solve the ecclesiastical confusion. This is because Scripture holds the final and authoritative answer on all of life's concerns. In fact, every question facing us today has two answers: God's answer and everyone else's. And when those two differ, everyone else is wrong.

Yet where do we often go for answers as a nation when there is chaos in our country? Where do we turn for solutions when we are experiencing moral, social, and economic decline at a rate that is able to destroy our country before our youngest generation even has a chance to grow up? What do we do when divisions, debt, and our own internal protests across our land threaten what little stability we have left?

What most Christians do, unfortunately, is change books. When it comes to politics and elections, far too many Christians spend more time appealing to family, history and tradition, culture, racial expediency, and personal preference than they do to what the Bible teaches. While most Christians verbally affirm Scripture is good enough for individuals, families, and churches, it seems that somehow it has been deemed insufficient for how we respond to politics and government.

Yet the same book that can restore a person, home, or church is the very same book that can restore and transform our nation. Friend, we don't need to change books. In fact, it is precisely because we have changed books that the chaos in our country has gotten worse than ever before.

It astounds me that in all the talk permeating the airwaves, around watercoolers, over dinners, and among Christian friends concerning the elections, candidates, parties, and platforms—how little a *biblically based* theistic worldview seems to enter the equation. God may get dropped in here or there on one issue, or perhaps two. But that is not good enough. Unless God and His revealed Word is the overarching influencer and rationale over how our electoral decisions are made as believers, then we cannot expect God to be the overarching influencer in our nation. Nor can we expect God to pour out His blessings on us as a country when He has been similarly marginalized, and at times even dismissed, from the political equation.

The same Bible that provides guidance and directions for how individuals, families, and churches ought to operate also gives clarity on how nations are to function politically.

While all the specific statutes and ordinances in Scripture given to Israel in the Old Testament do not automatically transfer to Gentile nations during this interim period known as the times of the Gentiles (Luke 21:24), the spirit of those laws, which are consistent with the character of God, does transfer since He is unchangeable in His essential nature, being, and attributes (Mal. 3:6; Heb. 13:8). This is especially true since the Old Testament was written for our example today (Rom. 15:4; 1 Cor. 10:6). Therefore, Gentile nations today can appropriately and relevantly apply the examples of divine principles from the Old Testament statutes and ordinances to contemporary political environments.

The greatest political statement in all of Scripture is the declaration of Revelation 19:16 that when Jesus Christ returns to earth to rule, He will come as King of kings and Lord of lords. He will be the visible ruler of the kings of the earth (Rev. 1:5). However, in the interim, He rules from His heavenly position; He is still sovereign over the kingdoms of this world (Col. 1:16–17). It is for this reason that kingdom-minded churches are to develop kingdom disciples who promote and advance a kingdom agenda in the political realm.

The kingdom agenda is defined as *the visible manifestation of the comprehensive rule of God over every area of life.* The glory of God and the advancement of His kingdom is the central theme of Scripture. This means that while there should be the institutional separation between church and state, there must never be the separation between the sacred and the secular or between God and politics. We should as kingdom citizens be seeking to mirror the governmental pattern of heaven into history through our righteous, political influence.

It's time for believers to make a radical return to God's Word as it relates to politics (and every other area for that matter). While we should do so with a respectful attitude, we must equally do so without apology. That is what this book is all about.

PART ONE

The Concept of Kingdom Politics

Chapter 1

THE RULER
OF THE NATIONS

We've all heard the nursery rhyme of Humpty Dumpty. It's about an egg who sat on a wall. And, as fate would have it, he had a great fall off that wall. While he sat up on that wall, he was on top of the world. He was doing okay. He had arrived at a precipice affording him a great and majestic view.

However, something went cataclysmically wrong for Mr. Dumpty. He fell off the wall. We don't have the particulars on what knocked him off. It could be that he was pushed, or maybe a gust of wind came along. Perhaps he got distracted and lost his balance. But what we do know is who he went to for help to try to get his life back on target. He didn't go to his family. He didn't go to his friends. He didn't go to the banker. Rather, he went to the White House. He went to the government.

The king got involved. He was so impacted by Mr. Dumpty's calamity that he called a meeting of Congress—all the king's men then got involved. Congress created and passed the "Fix Mr. Dumpty Law." I'm sure they also provided all the necessary funds and stimulus to put

Mr. Dumpty back together again. After all, it was widely known how shattered things had become.

All of this sounds like a solution up to this point. But the tragedy of the nursery rhyme is in how it concludes. All the king's horses and all the king's men did their best to put Humpty back together again. The most powerful people in the land, who had access to the greatest funding potential in society, were unable to fix the problem. Despite the valiant attempts to do good for Humpty, the egg remained cracked and broken. Apparently, a broken system was unable to fix a broken man whose world had been shattered.

It doesn't take a genius today to see that Humpty Dumpty remains shattered. In communities all over our nation and nations throughout the world, there is the shattering of hopes and dreams. There is a shattering of lives, communities, and property. Among this shattering, we face the inevitable uprising of class warfare, cultural warfare, and political warfare. Yet despite the funds to fix it, despite the responsibility to address it, all the king's horses and all the king's men have not been able to put Humpty Dumpty back together again.

Maybe it's because they really do not understand why Mr. Dumpty was broken in the first place. Maybe the politicians and the White House can't address the calamity and the brokenness successfully because they have been caught in what the Temptations used to sing—a "ball of confusion." In fact, that's what it seems the whole world is caught up in today. We have chaos on every continent and confusion in every nation. We have a global health pandemic, a racial pandemic, a spending pandemic, a debt pandemic, a military pandemic, and more wherever you look.

A SPIRITUAL PANDEMIC

Beneath these pandemics, though, lies the greatest pandemic of all. It's a spiritual pandemic. And if we don't get this one fixed right, then we won't have the cultural glue necessary to make Mr. Dumpty whole again. The Bible makes it clear that everything physical and visible is preceded by that which is invisible and spiritual. If you want to correct the physical and the visible, you must identify and address the invisible and spiritual. If all you see is what you see, you do not see all there is to be seen. The calamity we face today is because there has been an unaddressed spiritual issue, first and foremost by the church, which has then bled into the culture. If we fail to fix the spiritual, it doesn't matter how many king's horses and how many king's men attempt to help Mr. Dumpty's situation throughout our precious land.

This principle is made clear in 2 Chronicles 15:3–6 where we read,

> For many days Israel was without the true God and without a teaching priest and without law. But in their distress they turned to the LORD God of Israel, and they sought Him, and He let them find Him. In those times there was no peace to him who went out or to him who came in, for many disturbances afflicted all the inhabitants of the lands. Nation was crushed by nation, and city by city, for God troubled them with every kind of distress.

Please note that the chaos the nations were facing was caused by God Himself. This was the case because He had been marginalized by idolatry ("no true God"), there existed ecclesiastical failure ("no teaching priests"), and there was an absence of a fixed divine standard by which reality would be measured ("no law"). When nations depart from God, they face the consequences of God's divine passive wrath of abandonment. This results in nations, as well as their citizens, finding themselves experiencing the negative effects of evil, which then increasingly leads to the ongoing devolution of society. These nations experience an ever-rising amount of conflict personally, nationally, and internationally. Scripture is clear that God is the sovereign ruler over His creation (Ps. 96:10).

The biblical doctrine of sovereignty helps us grasp this truth more fully. Essentially, this doctrine makes it clear that God both rules and He overrules. Scripture is replete with this reality:

"But He is unique and who can turn Him?
And what His soul desires, that He does." (Job 23:13)

"I know that You can do all things,
And that no purpose of Yours can be thwarted." (Job 42:2)

Whatever the LORD pleases, He does,
In heaven and in earth, in the seas and in all deeps. (Ps. 135:6)

The LORD has made everything for its own purpose,
Even the wicked for the day of evil. (Prov. 16:4)

"Even from eternity I am He,
And there is none who can deliver out of My hand;
I act and who can reverse it?" (Isa. 43:13)

"The One forming light and creating darkness,
Causing well-being and creating calamity;
I am the LORD who does all these." (Isa. 45:7)

We have obtained an inheritance, having been predestined according to His purpose who works all things after the counsel of His will. (Eph. 1:11)

Then I heard something like the voice of a great multitude and like the sound of many waters and like the sound of mighty peals of thunder, saying,

"Hallelujah! For the Lord our God, the Almighty, reigns."
(Rev. 19:6)

So Pilate said to Him, "You do not speak to me? Do You not
know that I have authority to release You, and I have authority
to crucify You?" Jesus answered, "You would have no authority over Me, unless it had been given you from above; for this
reason he who delivered Me to you has the greater sin."
(John 19:10–11)

This sovereignty also includes God's rulership over nations as we
see here:

"It is He who changes the times and the epochs;
He removes kings and establishes kings;
He gives wisdom to wise men
And knowledge to men of understanding." (Dan. 2:21)

The king's heart is like channels of water in the hand of the
    Lord;
He turns it wherever He wishes. (Prov. 21:1)

And he said, "O Lord, the God of our fathers, are You not
God in the heavens? And are You not ruler over all the kingdoms of the nations? Power and might are in Your hand so
that no one can stand against You." (2 Chron. 20:6)

For the kingdom is the Lord's
And He rules over the nations. (Ps. 22:28)

When the spiritual is out of alignment, then the social, political, economic, technological, and environmental areas of life become

chaotic. The good news is that when people and nations return to God relationally under His kingdom rulership, He can bring order and peace to a chaotic environment (2 Chron. 15:4, 15).

That's why the story we read in Genesis 11 is so relevant not only to our contemporary culture but also to the world at large. God established national boundaries in which mankind is to live (Acts 17:26). This was God's way of subduing the world to His glory. At the Tower of Babel, men rebelled against God's plan for geographical decentralization by seeking to establish a unified global community independent of God. He judged their attempt at globalization independent of Him. If you've gone to church for any length of time, or have read your Bible, then you know this story. We're told in the opening verses that the whole earth used the same language at that time. God had given them an imperative through a divine instruction to scatter and "fill the earth" (Gen. 9:1). There was to be no globalization apart from Him, or one-world government independent of His sovereign rule. Rather, there was to be the breakdown of nations so that they would remain in a state of divine dependency on Him as the Creator, Controller, Sustainer, and Ruler of all nations, empires, and people (Acts 17:24–47).

But as the population began to grow, they did not seek to fulfill God's mandate of filling the earth. Instead, they chose to settle. We read,

Now the whole earth used the same language and the same words. It came about as they journeyed east, that they found a plain in the land of Shinar and settled there. (Gen. 11:1–2)

Let me start by saying a word about *east*. In the book of Genesis, to travel east meant to journey away from God. When Adam and Eve sinned, they were moved to the east (Gen. 3:24). When Cain was removed from the presence of God, he traveled east (Gen. 3:16). When the people and nations "journeyed east" in order to settle, they were moving away from God while simultaneously ignoring His mandate to populate the earth as distinct national entities (see Genesis 10).

Once they settled, they came up with an idea for how to create a place for them to live. We read in the next two verses,

> They said to one another, "Come, let us make bricks and burn them thoroughly." And they used brick for stone, and they used tar for mortar. They said, "Come, let us build for ourselves a city, and a tower whose top will reach into heaven, and let us make for ourselves a name, otherwise we will be scattered abroad over the face of the whole earth." (vv. 3–4)

God told them to scatter and cover the earth. But they opted for their own plan. They decided that rather than scatter their resources and strength abroad, they would consolidate their power. They wanted to consolidate their purpose by establishing their own civilization, culture, self-definition, and man-centered religious order. They wanted to build a global society that would erase the Creator-creature distinction and dependence.

In doing so, they wanted to remove the divine oversight of national identity and mandate that had been established, and enact their own rules for how civilization, culture, and government would operate. They wanted to set the rules and come up with their own plan. So they took the bricks combined with tar and set about creating a technology to do so. In that day, these building materials would have been their technology. It was what they had in order to advance civilization so that, in their minds at least, God would no longer be necessary. Theocracy (the rule of God) would be replaced by homocracy (the rule of man). Thus they began the plan to create their own Babel.

The citizens and government of Babel decided to pool their power and resources in order to build a world independent of divine structure. Keep in mind, whenever you use technology to create independence from God, you have joined the rebellion of Satan. In fact, governments that try to consolidate universal power are really joining Satan and the anti-Christ. According to Revelation 13:15–18, the system of the anti-Christ is predicated on the whole world economy being entwined. In this way, the anti-Christ would control it all and set up his own evil "kingdom" agenda (Isa. 14:12–14). His is an agenda independent of the directive God gave to create national dependency on Him.

To start, the inhabitants focused on building a city. This city would serve as the capital for the entire human race, since they had decided to settle in one area rather than disperse throughout the world. It was an effort to establish global unity independent of God's sovereign rule. Thus, they opted to build a civilization apart from God. We call that mindset *humanism*. Humanism is where man seeks to replace God in order to define life and its meaning, purpose, and responsibility on their own.

But since the leadership of the new civilization recognized the importance of religion, they decided to build a tower in the middle of the city. This tower would be known as a ziggurat and would serve as a staircase to heaven. They wanted this tower to help them establish a humanistic religious order that would satisfy the human need to believe in something bigger than themselves. They didn't want to look to God, but they wanted to become "god" by letting earth dictate to heaven. In this way they could focus on astrology or other interpretations of God's created order in an effort to define and direct their own paths. They wanted to define themselves by themselves as the objects of ultimate worship where mankind became the central connection between heaven and earth.

They wanted to create a doctrine that made belief in and submission to a sovereign God unnecessary, whether that was through evolution, or the spark of divinity, or materialism, greed, technology, or even medical advancement. They wanted to establish their own created order that left God out of His rightful position as ruler over all. And rather than connect with the Divine who comes from heaven to earth, they wanted to create their own religious connection from earth up to heaven. What's more, they wanted to be part of the applause when it was all said and done. They wanted their name carved onto a sign, into the building—to be remembered throughout all of history. As we saw in verse 4, they said, "And let us make for ourselves a name," so that they would not become scattered all over the earth. They thought that a one-world global community and government could eradicate the need for God because of the power of their collective unity.

In the context of Scripture, a name symbolizes a definition of what something is. To name something was akin to establishing governance over it. When God told Adam to name all the animals, God was setting Adam in a position of governance and responsibility over the animals that he named. That's one reason why God would change the name of a person who had changed their relationship to Him in Scripture. The name change signified a new identity and allegiance.

I've done my share of weddings over the years and in every wedding, the wife has changed her last name. It's a symbol of responsibility that the husband carries for the wife in order for him to properly govern her well-being. When the citizenry of Babel said they wanted to establish their own name, they were declaring their rebellion. They were declaring they wanted independence from God. They did not want to be defined or confined by a theocratic relationship with the Creator. Rather, they wanted a world they could run and own according to their own will and desires. They wanted to imitate God without yielding to Him.

What you and I are seeing today in our broken culture is a society that has been progressively imitating deity. We are witnessing a culture that has sought to define itself for itself, and not under God. Decisions and allegiances are made based on what people think, feel, or say and no longer based on God's solid Word. God rejects national and international covenants and alliances that leave Him out.

Children are being taught about self-definition in institutions where truth is jettisoned to the curb. Their understanding of *right* and *wrong* has been redefined. In fact, in so many situations what used to be "right" is now considered "wrong" and what used to be "wrong" is now considered "right" (Isa. 5:20). People are choosing their gender apart from what God has called them and created them. They choose their family structure apart from the way God intended the family to be. And they do this out of an illegitimate definition of freedom that they created themselves.

The problem is that regardless of what they think, say, or try to create, they are still dependent upon a Creator. If God were to simply reduce the oxygen flowing to any of their brains, the party would be over. Everything and everyone depends upon God. He is the Creator and Sustainer of all life. The most people can do apart from God is simply rearrange what He has already made. And whenever that takes place, it amounts to nothing more, and nothing less, than a cosmic rebellion. That can happen with an individual. It can happen with a rebellious family or a rebellious wife or a rebellious husband. It can happen with rebellious pastors. It can happen with rebellious politicians. It can happen with a rebellious president, and even with entire nations. You can pick the category yourself, but anytime someone seeks to place themselves in a position of governance outside of God's rule, it's rebellion. It is setting themselves up to make a name for themselves by demanding independence.

And while the people in Babel may have marveled at their own creation as their tower became taller and taller each day, it never grew so tall that God didn't have to come down in order to look at it Himself. Genesis 11:5 states it like this, "The LORD came down to see the city and the tower which the sons of men had built." God came down. Despite the fact that those building the tower stated that their goal was for it to reach clear to the heavens. Apparently, the heavens were out of reach for them because God still had to "come down" just to see what they were doing. Rather than invade God's space, as was their intention, God invaded theirs.

This is a great reminder for all of us. No matter how high any person or nation gets, it will never reach heaven. God sits high above the earth in a space humanity cannot reach, even with fancy spaceships or rockets. As the prophet Isaiah said, the nations are nothing before God (Isa. 40:15–24).

God came down to investigate what the people were doing in Babel, and when He did, He said, "Behold, they are one people, and they all have the same language. And this is what they began to do, and now nothing which they purpose to do will be impossible for them," (Gen. 11:6). This one statement by God is the single greatest testament to the power of unity. Here we see the Creator of the universe declaring that if the people stay together, they will be unstoppable. He said this because of the dominion mandate given in Genesis 1. When God delegated the rule of earth to mankind, it would be for good or ill. He determined to release humanity in such a way that our ability to rule could be great. If humanity rules under His overarching rule, He gives freedom. But if humanity chooses to rule independently of God, then the chaos they would invite would be like nothing they could imagine.

Thus, if God allowed humanity to become globally unified, independent of Him as God and Ruler over all, the rebellion and damage that would take place would be enormous. The chaos on earth would be unstoppable due to their sinful, anti-God global unity agenda. What we are witnessing today in America, and possibly even throughout the world (i.e., the United Nations), is what it looks like when humanity gets together in order to rebel against God. In fact, I'll go so far as to say that the United Nations is the contemporary expression of the Tower of Babel seeking to bring peace and international unity apart from the God of the Bible. International cooperation is one thing. Heading toward developing a global and one-world government is another. That's the spiritual pandemic in which we now find ourselves.

Rather than allow the self-perpetuated carnage to erupt from humanity's rebellion, God opted for a strategy to limit the scope of this initial rebellion. He gave that strategy in the next two verses of Genesis 11, which read,

> "Come, let Us go down there and confuse their language, so that they will not understand one another's speech." So the LORD scattered them abroad from there over the face of the whole earth; and they stopped building the city. (vv. 7–8)

God set in motion a "ball of confusion." He mixed things up so that there would not be any real, meaningful way to communicate. This was introduced in order to prevent the population from seeking to rebel collectively and thus invite unbridled calamity and destruction as a result of their departure from God.

Today we are experiencing the failure to communicate in any meaningful way among groups who are divided racially, politically, or through any number of ways. Sure, everyone is talking. But few are listening. The reason is because way back at Babel, God intentionally confused the language. It is something He has done and continues to do whenever any part or people or nation of His creation becomes too big for their britches. Any time a group rises up to declare themselves the rulers with final say apart from God's overarching rule, God allows the ball of confusion to do its work. He allows confusing and impossible situations to create panic. In this way, He seeks to remind them who is the ultimate Ruler over all.

As a result of confusing their language at Babel, God then scattered them all over the earth. In doing so, He fulfilled the mandate He had initially asked them to live out. God will accomplish His plan with or without our cooperation. His plan is for the church to serve as a model of what an individual nation should look like based on our biblical worldview and unity. We are to then seek to transfer a biblical worldview to other nations through the proclamation of the gospel, good works, and a comprehensive view of discipleship.

Let me just say it is better when we cooperate with God up front rather than forcing His hand in order to "come down" and intervene in our rebellion. He does this to force people and nations to have to learn to turn to Him. Believers are commanded to disciple the nations, not just individuals in the nations. This involves impacting and affecting the systems and structures that affect the nations (Matt. 28:19).

God is not shy on where to place blame for the consequences of humanity's rebellion. Twice in the passage in Genesis 11 He tells us that it is "the LORD" who scattered them all over the earth. He didn't want us to miss that if you mess with Him, it comes at a price. And if you and I want to honestly know why we have the problems we are facing in our world today—why we can't seem to fix the social crisis, the racial crisis, the health crisis—we may want to take a look at "the LORD." Because if God is our problem, then only God is our solution. We can make all the mandates, precautions, sensitivity classes, economic stimulus packages, and international summits that we want, but if it is a spiritual root that is rotting, we need to return to God in order to solve the issues at hand. God will not allow our nation, or any nation, to solve its problems simply by political alliances. While national cooperation is legitimate, globalization and one-world cooperation apart from God is not.

God had given the people a choice before they began to build their tower. He had given them an option to scatter and fill the earth on their own or reject His directive and He would scatter them as a result. But they decided to think more highly of themselves than they ought, so they opted for settling instead. Yet when God came down to see what they were doing and He jumbled up their language and stifled their economy, the people had to stop building. God halted their progress, since they weren't able to work together anymore. He brought an end to their unity so that they were now fighting against each other because they couldn't communicate. In fact, God shut the whole rebellious plan down. And He wasn't shy about letting them know it was He who did it.

You and I have a decision to make in our land right now. We can either continue in the rebellious trend of our nation apart from God's rule and His favor, or we can challenge our political leaders to return to God willingly and help bring healing to our land. Whether we do it willingly or whether God has to come down and intervene in order to get us right with Him, He will accomplish His goal for His creation. If we choose to cooperate with the process, there will be less chaos along the way. If we don't, we only need to turn on the evening news to see the ongoing results of having it our own way. God still rules the nations.

God is speaking to all nations right now through the various issues we are facing head on. He is telling us that our power can't fix this problem. Through allowing an international, medical pandemic (COVID-19) to affect the whole world, God has clearly demonstrated that He is indeed Ruler of the nations. He is reminding us that money and power can't fix these problems. He is letting us know that notoriety and celebrity won't fix these issues once He decides to move. The reason is because only God can fix what needs to be fixed in our land. Until we figure that out and come right with God as kingdom followers seeking to elect and enact kingdom-based politicians and policies, we can expect a zillion other options of disturbance on our common goals. God won't accept national or global unity apart from Him. He calls for unity that is centered around and stems from Him.

God's goal is for an international theocracy under the lordship of Jesus Christ (Ps. 2:1–12; 1 Cor. 15:24–25). Until then, God will not allow unbelievers to form a world coalition independent of Him. Yet unfortunately, as we have seen, we have lost God as a nation and international community. We have lost the very connection we have to purpose, meaning, and progress. As a result, everything seems out of order. Everything seems challenging at best. Everything is off. It doesn't make sense. The only way for us to experience redemption as a country and peace in our land is in returning to God. He is not far if we will just recognize His sovereign rule (Acts 17:27).

God wants nations to run back to Him. He wants us to find Him. He wants us to turn from our wicked ways and acknowledge His rightful rule over our lives and societies. God Himself has created a divine disruption because He is giving us a chance for a divine reset. We had better take advantage of this opportunity to return to Him while we still have time so we can advance His kingdom agenda throughout the world. We do this by pursuing a relationship with Him that includes submitting to His ultimate rule. God has been and always will be the Ruler of the nations and He desires that all nations, languages, and people groups praise Him (Rev. 7:9; Ps. 2:10–12).

May God give us another chance as a nation to rally around His kingdom purposes, and may He deliver healing in our land.

Chapter 2

THE LINK BETWEEN GOD AND GOVERNMENT

E very day at Alexander Hamilton Elementary School in Baltimore, Maryland, where I grew up, the teacher would have all the students stand. He or she would then have us place our hands over our hearts and recite the Pledge of Allegiance. Together we would state the familiar words:

> *I pledge allegiance to the flag of the United States of America, and to the Republic for which it stands, one nation, under God, indivisible with liberty and justice for all.*

In that urban Baltimore school, I was reminded day in and day out that we were to recommit ourselves to fidelity to the nation. This pledge served as a verbal covenantal commitment to the country.

You might be surprised to learn that this concept of a national covenant—an agreement to commit yourself to the well-being of the nation, as well as declare receptivity for the benefits that accrue to you from that country—is not an American concept. It is a biblical concept. The Scripture itself endorses covenants.

In fact, in God's kingdom, He has four covenantal relationships. These are:

1. Personal Covenant (where you pledge fidelity to Him as an individual)
2. Family Covenant (where a couple and family place themselves under His rule)
3. Church Covenant (where a body of believers declare loyalty and alignment to Him)
4. National Covenant (where a country pledges to exist as one nation under God)

In this last covenant, there would be an assumption that if the nation remained undivided, functioning as one, then it would similarly be filled with both liberty and justice for every citizen. To put it another way, if God was not a part of the equation for a nation, then not only would unity be in trouble, but also justice and liberty. This would be due to the nation's departure from a covenantal alignment under our Creator.

A *covenant* is *a divinely created relational bond*. It exists as an agreement between any of the above-mentioned entities and God. The benefit of this covenant is that those who align under God will be covered by God, because a covenant is designed to provide covering and social advancement (Deut. 29:9).

A covenant is like an umbrella. An umbrella doesn't stop it from raining, it just stops the rain from reaching you. The umbrella covers you so that you do not have to experience the effects of the rain on you. Similarly, God covers those who are in covenant with Him. He doesn't stop the storms or calm all chaos, but what He does is provide covering in the midst of it.

God made it clear in Psalm 33:12 that a nation is blessed when they recognize Him as God over them. It says, "Blessed is the nation whose God is the LORD, the people whom He has chosen for His own inheritance." The nation who recognizes God as Lord will find His favor. It doesn't say the nation who simply recognizes the person of God, but also the position of God, as "LORD." That is, to recognize His rule and His policies in how a nation is to function. When that is done consistently, the nation itself receives God's blessings. Likewise, when that is not done or when God is rejected as ruler and Lord, then the nation itself loses out on the blessings of God (Jer. 18:7–12).

This is why it is incumbent upon Christians first and foremost to ascribe ourselves not first to a political party but rather to the superintending governance of God through the mechanism of civil government. No political party fully represents the values of the king-dom of God. It is to the degree that we operate under this covenantal umbrella through aligning our actions and policies under God that we will experience the goodness of God in our land. In this manner, we will also encourage the goodness and righteousness in those who rule our land.

Civil government that is rightly related to God should mirror His trinitarian nature of unity and diversity. Within the Godhead, there is unity of purpose and authority but not sameness of function (i.e., the three branches of government). Governments should reflect this reality as a constitutional republic administered through its just and righteous representatives that consistently reflect biblical standards.

Scripture makes it clear in Romans 13:1 that we are to submit to governing authorities. It says, "Every person is to be in subjection to the governing authorities. For there is no authority except from God, and those which exist are established by God." Therefore, whoever resists authority has opposed the ordinance of God. In doing so, they similarly usher in condemnation upon themselves.

This is why we must seek the right kind of government according to the will of God. Since we are called to submit to governing authorities, we must do everything we can to ensure God remains in the equation when it comes to our policies and governmental structures and leadership. The further you remove God's person and His policies from politics, the further you remove the nation from a position of blessing, power, and covering. You leave the nation exposed to all manner of attack, vulnerabilities, destruction, and infiltration.

No matter how much you pray as a nation or how much you use God's name or appeal to His mercy, if God has been removed from how a government functions, the character of its leaders and the values of its citizens, those prayers will often go unanswered. Leaving God out of the equation also removes God's intervention and blessing on the nation. God's principles are never to be separated from the overarching governance of a land.

In fact, the Bible is pregnant with politics. From Genesis to Revelation, you see God involved with politics. We read about Him establishing or dismantling governments, giving standards for laws or judging lawbreakers. God is not disengaged when it comes to nations and politics. He makes His rule a comprehensive statement over "all authorities," not just some. He is to be over the mayor, city council, state legislature, governor, house of representatives, senate, president, and more. God rules over all.

To the degree that these various authorities are aligned with God's person and His policies is to that degree that the nation experiences unity, justice, and liberty. Conversely, to the degree that these various authorities are unaligned with God's person and His policies is to that degree that chaos will consume order.

As we move forward in our journey exploring kingdom politics and how this concept relates to politics in America, or in any nation, we must look at the role of civil government from a biblical perspective. With any subject, we should always start with the Bible and what God has to say on the matter.

According to Romans 13, the biblical role of civil government is *to maintain a safe, just, righteous, and compassionately responsible environment for freedom to flourish.* I'll talk more on what biblical freedom means later in this book, but for now just know that biblical freedom can be defined as *the unimpeded opportunity and responsibility to choose to righteously, justly, and legally pursue one's divinely created reason for being.* This means that civil government is to protect its citizens from enemies within (public safety) and enemies without (i.e., national defense) while establishing righteous laws based on God's standard so that people can be unencumbered in their desire, determination, and ability to pursue their God-given potential. All of this should be done in an environment of compassion, responsibly administering to the poor.

The freedom that is actualized through a kingdom perspective on politics, that of embracing God's sovereignty and rule over all authorities, generates a faith more powerful than any human weapon or system of philosophy could ever produce. It accesses God's grace in such a way as to grant a freedom that is not dependent upon externals. This is the only true, authentic freedom as it manifests God's ability to bring about good in any and every situation surrendered to Him.

You cannot remove God's perspective from government, especially His perspective on freedom, and have an ordered society. Without God's rule and perspective both to guide and to govern, a nation will devolve into chaos and anarchy. It will become an oppressive society simultaneously adhering to a freedom that has no standards. This double-mindedness opens the door for all manner of mistreatment or manipulation based on the whim of the moment.

I'm certain I've ruffled some feathers already by starting out so strongly on the connection of God with government. Especially since we live in a culture that emphasizes the separation of church and state.

But keep in mind, the separation of church and state is not the same thing as the connection of God and government. I'm not purporting a national theocracy in examining the scriptural emphasis on God's involvement with politics. The reason I'm not purporting it is because the Bible already declares that the world is a theocracy. That's a given. We read in Psalm 22:28, "For the kingdom is the LORD's and He rules over the nations." God is already ruling over everything. What ought to concern us, and what the separation of church and state addresses, is that of an *ecclesiocracy*. This is when a particular institutionalized religion governs a society.

Unfortunately, in our effort to defend against organized religion and its potential governmental rule, we have also pushed God's rightful rule, His universal theocracy, out the window. Yet whenever a society removes God and His influence from its midst, you wind up with a *homocracy* whereby mankind seeks to replace God in the name of government (i.e., statism). If societies refuse to rule by God and His principles, then they will inevitably be ruled by men and civil structures that will seek to be God.

When we choose to leave God and the dominant perspectives of the nation, both the government and its citizens will be at risk. If you and I want to live in a country flourishing in the areas of safety, justice, righteousness, and compassion, we will have to align ourselves under God Himself. I didn't say that we need to align ourselves under religion, or under a denomination, or even under religious leaders. But we do need to align ourselves under God's rule and His perspective on all subjects. Simply stated, the closer a nation is to God's person and principles, the more ordered that society will be. The further that nation is from God and His principles, the more chaotic and oppressive that society will become.

The idea of government is to mirror, or reflect, the image of God for the well-being of society. When God established the nation of Israel, He gave them a constitution. We refer to this constitution as the Ten Commandments. This is one reason why you will often see the Ten Commandments in a courthouse in our nation because these commands established the boundaries of the governing rule of the land and restricted the evil of its citizens (1 Tim. 1:8–10).

In addition to the Ten Commandments, God also gave them 613 statutes and ordinances. These provided the framework for which the application of the Ten Commandments would be carried out in society. Deuteronomy 29:9 tells us that God declared when Israel and her citizenry would abide by these laws, they would be blessed.

In this inception of governance, God gave us the formula for how even Gentile nations obtain His blessings or judgments as a nation (Gen. 18:20–33; Ezek. 25–32). Thus, if we really want to see our nation healed and helped, we need to re-insert God's person and perspective into politics. Once He is excluded—which He has been to a large degree at this time in history—that vacuum will be filled with that which will destroy a nation. Romans 1:18–32 explains how this happens. The bottom line is that when the people no longer wanted to "retain the knowledge of God," or operate according to His perspective, God "turned them over" to depravity and its resultant effects of decay. That is, they experience the consequences of divine abandonment due to their idolatry. Idolatry is where right and wrong is determined apart from God.

If we are tired of witnessing decay in our land, we need to make it a higher priority to emphasize God's perspective in political discussions and actions. Whether politicians are Democrats or Republicans, they are to govern according to God's perspective on whatever the issue is. As long as the enemy can keep us illegitimately divided, whether by making us more Democrat than Christian, or more Republican than Christian, then we are aiding and abetting the deterioration and the destruction of the culture.

Government is not only a political enterprise. Government is a sacred enterprise, because it was initiated by God. It is a spiritual enterprise. What discourages me so much during seasons of political discourse is that when the spiritual is brought up, people, including many Christians, get offended. They don't seem to want to hear what God has to say about justice or righteousness or life or liberty. In fact, not too long ago one of our congressmen, Florida Representative Greg Steube, chose to read from my Bible commentary about what the Word of God says on the subject of gender identity. At the end of his reading, Rep. Jerry Nadler responded by saying, "Mr. Steube, what any religious tradition ascribes as God's will is no concern of this Congress."[1]

Since government was established and created by God as part of His covenantal rule over His creation, and since He alone is the standard by which laws are right and wrong (James 4:12), what He says on any and every subject ought to be the highest concern of Congress. People and politicians may have opinions that disagree with God's Word, but when they do, it is they who need to adjust. God does not adjust His righteous and just standards for anyone. Only when a government submits to God's governance can it hope to be rescued (Isa. 33:22).

But the mere fact that we have elected leaders solemnly declaring that God's will has no place in Congress is a testament to why our nation is in the level of sheer chaos, violence, injustices, and debt we see today. Daniel 5:21 says, "The Most High God is ruler over the realm of mankind and *that* He sets over it whomever He wishes."

When our kids were at home, they would often bring in ideas and suggestions for alterations to rules that went against mine. But as the "president" of my home and my family, I would remind them

---

1. "Rep. Jerry Nadler: 'What Any Religious Tradition Ascribes as God's Will Is No Concern of This Congress,'" CNSNews.com, March 1, 2021, https://www .cnsnews.com/article/washington/cnsnewscom-staff/rep-jerry-nadler-what-any- religious-tradition-ascribes-gods. Rep. Steube had quoted from *The Tony Evans Bible Commentary* (Nashville, TN: Holman Reference, 2019), 231.

that their ideas were not the final say. They would bring in their perspectives, but the ultimate decision remained with me. That would inevitably create a conflict between myself and them, but it would soon be resolved when I reminded them that if they didn't want to abide by my rules, they could buy their own home and set their own rules. This world is God's creation. This is His house. His rules will stand. It doesn't matter if peer pressure or sinful desires cause a myriad of people to rise up and declare that other rules should be installed. God is the One who sits over all, and He is the One to determine how things are to run. Now, if we as a people choose to go against His rules, then we will pay the piper.

When we formed our nation, we declared that we would operate as "one nation under God." We acknowledged that this was God's house. Those who founded our nation may not have lived up to or by His standards in all things, as is obvious when it comes to slavery, but the awareness of the higher standard was established. God is calling us as a nation of citizens to recognize His rule over all. He is calling us to live according to His standards of good and evil. Our nation and our politicians are to seek to reward good behavior while punishing evil behavior. Romans 13 puts it like this,

> For rulers are not a cause of fear for good behavior, but for evil. Do you want to have no fear of authority? Do what is good and you will have praise from the same; for it is a minister of God to you for good. But if you do what is evil, be afraid; for it does not bear the sword for nothing; for it is a minister of God, an avenger who brings wrath on the one who practices evil. Therefore it is necessary to be in subjection, not only because of wrath, but also for conscience' sake. (vv. 3–5)

God alone defines what makes good laws and is good behavior and what is evil (Ezek. 44:24; Ezra 7:25–26). That's what the Ten

Commandments did. They set the standard under which all would fall. If people and politicians would learn to operate by the rules of engagement that God has freely made known, our nation would take on a different template. If our leaders used their positions to bring about justice and righteousness, as God defines it, in order to promote unity, we would experience the freedom and divine covering God offers a nation as He defines it.

The Bible tells us in Deuteronomy 4:8 that nations become great when they follow God's righteous laws. If we are going to invite in help and healing in our country, we need to strive toward enacting and following God's righteous laws. God is so entwined with the governing of a nation that Scripture even refers to politicians as "ministers of God." The term *minister* is mostly used to refer to preachers or church leaders in our country today. But from a biblical context, a minister of God is also someone who is a civil servant. There are some nations today who still reference their politicians as "ministers" in their titles. This is because government and the structure of government originates with God and is designed to serve its citizens in God's name.

Those who govern in politics are to reflect God's values in reinforcing good behavior and policing against evil. Roman soldiers were considered the policemen of the day in biblical times. As part of their uniform, they would carry a sword. The sword was for two things. The first was to intimidate. The goal in intimidation would be to limit potential bad behavior from taking place before it even got started. But the second reason the Roman soldiers carried the sword was for judgment, which included capital punishment (Gen. 9:6). Whether it was evil by the citizens or by the leaders, the sword was a tool of intimidation and judgment. It meant that evil would not go ignored.

This was their way of maintaining a safe and just environment for the people. Freedom cannot flourish in any nation apart from safety. Freedom cannot flourish in any nation apart from justice and righteousness. Freedom flourishes when governments rule according to God's standards. And when they do not, it is our role as believers in the body of Christ to pray for them. In fact, we are to pray for politicians and civil servants as a regular part of our prayer life (1 Tim. 2:2). It is also our responsibility to respectfully challenge them when they clearly deviate from God's standards (1 Sam. 15:10–23; Matt. 14:1–4).

If you have ever watched the movie *Inception*, you'll remember the spinning top. The film is about a man who goes into other people's dreams to figure out what they are thinking based on what they are dreaming. Because he enters dreamland so often, he needs a tool to indicate when he is dreaming and when he is not. To help him identify what is real and what is a dream, he has a spinning top. If the top keeps spinning, he knows he is in a dream. If the top starts wiggling and wobbling and falls over, he knows he is in real time and space. In other words, there is so much confusion and chaos coming at him that he needs an objective standard outside of himself to tell him what is real and what isn't.

We're living in a land of inception right now. We're living in a quasi-dreamland state where confusion and chaos keep us from knowing which way we are coming or going. There is so much deception prevalent in our world today that it is difficult to know what or who to believe. Up means down. Right means left. Good means bad. Things have gotten twisted, and it is difficult to identify where we are and where we need to go. That's why we all need a tool. We need something to help us discriminate and discern through all the muck and the mire of the political mess. Our tool has to be the divine standard of the Word of God.

The first question we must always ask publicly on any subject, policy, politician, or direction is what does God say about it? What does His Scripture declare? In going to Scripture first, you are affirming God's rightful place as sovereign ruler over all. He rules the nations and their leaders (Prov. 8:15). It is He who sets the standard.

It is He who speaks on how to execute judgment in such a way as to curtail its further spread in the culture (Eccl. 8:11).

Our problem today is that our people and our politicians have sought to usurp God's rightful role as Potentate over our land. That would be similar to football players or basketball players deciding they also want to be the referees. The game would come to a swift end.

There is not one issue in government or politics to which God has not given a precept or a principle on how it should be viewed and governed. Yet when people scramble to form their own rules, they are walking on a tightrope and doing so as if they were blind. As Isaiah 8:20 says, "If they do not speak according to this word, it is because they have no dawn." In other words, they can't see straight. There appears to be a lot of blindness right now when it comes to the issues of justice, immigration, taxation, foreign relations, sanctity of life, gender, morality, family, and so much more. God has spoken on all these subjects, and He has not stuttered. It's all in His Word.

God must be included in government in order to have government function in the way God designed it to function. He must be included if a government is going to promote good and keep evil from proliferating. Psalm 72:11 says, "And let all kings bow down before him, all nations serve him." Last I checked, *all* still means *all*.

Our nation has devolved in so many ways that we must rise up and promote God's standards once again. This is not a time for cute Christianity. This is not a time for popular politics. It's not a time to placate the masses. This is the time for Christians to take their stand.

If we are to ever become unified as the body of Christ, we will make a difference. We will have an influence. We will bring about good in a nation that desperately needs it. But we will only do this when we start to bring in our biblical worldview to the ballot box, and everywhere else.

When we decide to take God's rule seriously, we will lead the way on the issues that plague us as a nation. Ineffective Christians are one of the major problems in our country today because we have been Christian in name, not in action. We have not been kingdom-minded. We've given in to the pressure and have become more culturally minded or politically minded and thus we have contributed to the chaos of the culture. But now is the time, in the midst of the chaos, to step forward and set things straight.

We will look at this passage in greater depth later, but in Genesis 11, we read how God allowed there to be confusion in the land. The people declared in both word and action that they wanted a society without Him and so God let them have it. He let them experience the confusion and the chaos that comes as part of that choice.

We're seeing something very similar in our nation today. Far too many people are seeking to remove God's rule so that we are no longer "one nation under God." But when we remove "under God," you will discover that we are a nation who has gone under.

If you and I want to see our nation healed and helped, we must not extract God from government anymore. It is His rule which is to rule over all.

Chapter 3

THE FOUNDATION OF FREEDOM

A t the core of this book rests the foundational truth that God promises to bless the nation that prioritizes His relationship to them. When we recognize this reality, our perspectives on politics should shift. Our strategy for how our nation operates will work best when it is aligned under God's overarching principles.

When we stray from His values, we stray from His blessing, protection, and covering.

As a refresher, the biblical definition for civil government is *to maintain a safe, just, righteous, and compassionately responsible environment for freedom to flourish.* After all, freedom is the hallmark of our homeland. As the Statue of Liberty proclaims while she prominently stands in the New York Harbor:

Give me your tired, your poor,
Your huddled masses yearning to breathe free,
The wretched refuse of your teeming shore.

Send these, the homeless, tempest-tossed to me,
I lift my lamp beside the golden door![2]

At her base is a broken chain because this would symbolize in principle the place where people could find the pathway to freedom. Freedom, and liberty, are valuable to the human race. Without them, a person's life is bound to the will of another and often, as a result, exploited. Thus, since civil government's primary role is to ensure this flourishing of freedom in our land by providing a safe, just, and compassionate environment in which it can be experienced, we need to explore in greater detail how that is effectively done.

Just because a nation declares freedom and justice for all does not mean that freedom and justice for all is lived out. In fact, I recently filmed a Bible study on race relations and racial history in front of the Liberty Bell in Philadelphia. The reason why this location was chosen was due to the contradictory nature of this bell. On one hand, the Liberty Bell signifies freedom and liberty for America's citizens. On the other hand, it was crafted and erected at a time when freedom and liberty were denied to the majority of black people living in the nation. The crack on the bell reflects more than imperfections in its materials, it also reflects imperfections in the living out of its message.

In order to fully realize and actualize the freedom we are intended to have and benefit from in our country, we will need to look at what freedom is and how it applies to humanity. Keep in mind this important truth: you and I don't get to define freedom, since we didn't create it. Our government leaders don't get to define freedom either, since they didn't create it. Neither do our founding fathers get to define freedom since they, also, did not create it. The first use of the concept of freedom did not occur in the American Constitution.

2. Emma Lazarus, "The New Colossus," *The Poems of Emma Lazarus* (United States: Houghton, Mifflin, 1888).

The first use occurred in the Word of God.

Therefore, in order to truly understand freedom and how it is to be applied in a nation, we must find out what God has to say about it. As a theologian, I was taught early on in hermeneutics to apply an approach to studying God's Word that is called the law of first mention. This simply means that if you want to determine the meaning of a term or concept in Scripture, you look at the context of when it was first introduced. You then apply this meaning as a foundational definition throughout the various ways it is used elsewhere in the Bible, unless the Bible itself gives you permission to change it. If we were to utilize this study tool when it comes to the concept of freedom, we would need to go all the way back to the beginning. We would need to look at Genesis 2:15–17 to discover how God introduced this term to us initially. We read,

> Then the LORD God took the man and put him into the garden of Eden to cultivate it and keep it. The LORD God commanded the man, saying, "From any tree of the garden you may eat freely; but from the tree of the knowledge of good and evil you shall not eat, for in the day that you eat from it you will surely die."

As you can see, the principle of freedom was tied to the creation of humanity. When God created the first man, Adam, who would serve as the preamble for the human race, He introduced this crucial issue we call freedom. Since God created it and inserted it into our world, we should abide by His definition of it.

Unfortunately, though, we live in a world today populated by those who wish to define freedom differently than God. But God has already said what He meant. He didn't give us a basis for changing what He said nor what He meant when He said it.

It is important to notice that in God's first introduction and definition of the concept of freedom, He gave the scope of freedom. He did this when He let Adam know that he could eat from every tree in the garden. This range gave a broad scope of freedom to humanity at the outset. Humanity was given a choice. We were given the opportunity to choose from God's bountiful provision because everything God had made by that time was good.

As you can see, God's definition of freedom *is the unimpeded opportunity and responsibility to choose to righteously, justly, and legally pursue one's divinely created reason for being.* It is where you get to choose from what God has provided for you in order to maintain and maximize His created order.

The principle of broad freedom, while introduced in Genesis at the beginning of known time, is echoed throughout Scripture. Leviticus 25:10 states it like this,

> "You shall thus consecrate the fiftieth year and proclaim a release through the land to all its inhabitants. It shall be a jubilee for you, and each of you shall return to his own property, and each of you shall return to his family."

God declares in the jubilee that they were to proclaim liberty throughout the land. Liberty is freedom. The jubilee principle of freedom was reiterated by Jesus (Luke 4:18–19). This is why when you see governments that are oppressive, or that seek to reduce and restrict freedom illegitimately, you'll also see the culture of the government trying to marginalize, dumb down, or control religion, the church, and God. The reason for this is because God's view of freedom—free will, personal choice, and autonomy under His overarching rule—means that government agencies are not in ultimate control. God is. God gives each of us the opportunity to make personal choices. Yes, we each also have to live with the consequences of those choices, but we have the right to choose within His sovereign boundaries of life.

That's why freedom is so magnificent because we have been given so many things to choose from. Freedom involves being released from anything or anybody holding you illegitimately hostage from what God has authorized for you to enjoy and benefit from in what He has provided.

And while freedom involves choice (Deut. 30:19), it also involves responsibility. God put Adam in the garden "to cultivate it and keep it." God gave Adam freedom, but in that freedom He also gave him a role. Adam was designated the responsibility to manage, maintain, and expand the productivity in his sphere of influence. What God established with Adam would be the preamble for governing later on based on His government in the garden. If Adam chose to act responsibly related to the good things that God had provided, he had the opportunity to take, use, expand, and benefit from all that God had created. He also had the ability to enjoy it because we can see in the passage that the fruit was sweet to the taste.

Freedom is to be utilized and enjoyed. It is to be benefited from both individually and collectively. God allows each of us, in the name of freedom, to maximize our potential. And since His initial governing guidelines were to be the preamble for future governing guidelines, all governments ought also to be designed to allow people to maximize their freedom. Which is why governments often seek to get rid of God—they hold you hostage and want to be your god.

God gives broad scope to the concept of freedom. But He doesn't give it without limitations. God's definition of freedom comes with restrictions as well, but they are narrow. You will recall from the passage in Genesis when God introduced Adam to the garden that He did give Adam one restriction. We read,

> Then the LORD God took the man and put him into the garden of Eden to cultivate it and keep it. The LORD God commanded the man, saying, "From any tree of the garden

you may eat freely; but from the tree of the knowledge of good and evil you shall not eat, for in the day that you eat from it you will surely die." (Gen. 2:15–17)

God created a limitation within the opportunity for broad freedom. We can consider it like a boundary. In doing so, He established His rule and authority as the final rule and authority humanity was to operate by. Maximizing your freedom under God demands legitimate boundaries. The boundaries are not designed to restrict freedom but rather to enhance it. Like a red light providing a boundary for oncoming traffic, the limitation exists to allow a greater amount of freedom for all traffic. Because if there were no boundaries in driving, driving would be far more dangerous and costly to anyone and everyone taking part. By issuing legitimate boundaries, the actual experience of freedom is enhanced.

For example, a football player cannot run up into the stands or the concession area and come back down to the field and finish a play. He can't run out one tunnel and circle around in the parking lot and enter the other tunnel only to declare he's scored a touchdown. That's not football. That's chaos. If that were football, then it would have no fans. No players. No referees. No stadiums. This is because no one would pay attention to that which was a mere mess, and thus football would lose its source of funding and close down. Players are only free to play football when they operate within the boundaries.

Another sport, tennis, has a base line. A tennis player can't hit the ball into the stands and claim a point. In order to enjoy the freedom of both playing or watching tennis, the players must function within the restrictions of the lines. Baseball has a foul line. You get the point.

Did you know that a fish can't last long out of water because they have been created and designed to function and be free in the environment and boundary of water? Similarly, you and I can't live long underwater because we were created and designed to function and be free in a different environment. If a person remains too long underwater, he or she will drown.

A train is not free to take you from one city to another in any which way the conductor chooses. The train must carry its passengers on the track it's designed for. The moment the conductor turns the train to go out across the prairie is the moment the train has lost its own freedom because it can no longer go at all. It will have crashed and failed to live up to its designer's purpose.

In order for freedom to be experienced, enjoyed, and benefited from, boundaries must exist. The goal of freedom is to maximize the reason why you were created in the first place. Yet what we see happening around us today is people wanting to be free *from* their created purpose, not *for* their created purpose. They want to be free outside of God's limited restrictions, which then leads to anarchy, chaos, and confusion in society and the world.

God gave Adam free access to all the trees, except for one. He provided maximum freedom with limited regulations. Essentially, God told Adam he could have what he wanted but he was not to mess with the Google Tree in the middle. He wasn't to touch the Information Center, also known as the "tree of the knowledge of good and evil" that sat in the middle of the garden. That was his only restriction. Yet the Google Tree proved to be too much of a temptation, so he eventually ate from it, as we know all too well.

If I were to contemporize the placement of the tree a bit, I could say that it was put in the living room or the den of a home. The garden would signify the entire house, but the living room was the main, central area of the house. Whenever Adam went to his bedroom, he would have to pass through the living room. Or when he went to the kitchen, he could look out and see the living room. Everywhere Adam went, he would constantly be reminded of the one Information Center available to him by means of access but not available to him by means of authority. It was this one tree he was told to leave alone.

The reason that God put the tree in the living room was to remind Adam who was in charge. He wanted to give Adam maximum freedom without a litany of rules, but He also wanted to keep a reminder front and center for Adam that neither he nor his progeny was the ultimate creator of all. He might have the ability to name the creation, but never in a million years could he recreate creation. That is God's role, and this is God's world. And because it is God's world, He wants us to operate and function according to His knowledge, not according to human reason. We are to live by divine revelation, not our own finite understanding.

In other words, we are to get our instruction from God. We are not to come up with it on our own, apart from Him. While He's given us freedom, which always comes with a choice, He wants to remind us that it's not in our best interest to experience this freedom our own way independent of Him. It remains in our best interest to maximize and experience our freedom under God's overarching kingdom rule. When you and I do that, and when governments allow for that, we will know what it truly means to live with the benefits and enjoyment of freedom.

When God established the entity known as government, He created it with the idea of limited regulations. We witness this first and foremost in the governance set forth in the garden. But we also witness it when we look at how God established the nation of Israel. Israel was established in the format for how a society is supposed to run and how civil government is supposed to function. When we think in terms of Israel as a nation and its government, most of us tend to reflect on the Ten Commandments, as we should. These ten commandments established the non-negotiable boundaries for how a civil society should run. They were specific in nature, but they were also limited in scope. There were just these ten things to live according to in order to have a free society where everyone could fully maximize his or her potential.

What's more, when God introduced the Ten Commandments,

He did so with a statement that many people miss. He provides the context for the commandments in His opening line, which is, "I am the LORD your God, who brought you out of the land of Egypt, out of the house of slavery" (Ex. 20:2). In this revealing opening statement, God reminds the people of Israel that He is the one who gave them their freedom in the first place. He is the one who set them free from the land of Egypt and their house of slavery. Thus, since He provided the freedom, He has the right to set the boundaries in which they were to function. Said boundaries were designed to create opportunity for citizens to take full advantage of freedom.

God gave commandments that, as I mentioned earlier, led to 613 statutes and ordinances on how to apply the Ten Commandments in society. He did this to demonstrate that if they applied the ten rules as indicated, they would live in a free society. They would live with the freedom for why He created government and why He created civilization and nations. Yet the moment these commandments and the principles behind them or the principles behind the regulations are inconsistent in the governing authorities of a land, there will be problems. There will be chaos and violence. The reason is because God has established His rules in order that society and her citizens can function to its fullest.

Civil government has been designed to function, as well as to enforce the functioning of her citizens, according to these principles. In 1 Samuel 8:10–19, the passage goes into greater detail on how excluding God and His principles from government is dangerous for citizens, as well as describing how the government should function and what laws it is to enact. We see this in the repeated use of the word *take* throughout the passage. When the people of Israel called out for their own king apart from the leadership God had appointed over them, the prophet Samuel warned them about what would happen. A few of these warnings include (bold added):

"He will **take** your sons and place them for himself." (v. 11)

"He will also **take** your daughters for perfumers and cooks and bakers." (v. 13)

"He will **take** the best of your fields and your vineyards and your olive groves." (v. 14)

"He will **take** a tenth of your seed and of your vineyards." (v. 15)

"He will also **take** your male servants and your female servants and your best young men and your donkeys." (v. 16)

"He will **take** a tenth of your flocks, and you yourselves will become his servants." (v. 17)

After indicating everything the king and his new government would take, which was a lot, as you can see, God foreshadowed what the people would then do. He let them know through Samuel,

"Then you will cry out in that day because of your king whom you have chosen for yourselves, but the LORD will not answer you in that day." (v. 18)

God made it clear in their request for a king outside of His own ruling authority that if they were to build a civil government apart from Him establishing the rules, that civil government would set out to take from them what they valued the most, and would force them to participate in wars they may not have had any business being a part of. That civil government would require illegitimate taxes that they would be obligated to pay. The government would influence and control their children, their businesses, their flocks, and much more. The reason for the all-out control would be as a result of turning their government into their god.

The Israelites saw the neighboring nations who were ruled by kings, and they wanted the same protection they felt the other nations were getting. Rather than trust in God and His methods, they sought to do things like everyone else. But God was reminding them before they made that decision that once they started to look to government as a god rather than to God, the government would then insert itself into every aspect and fiber of their being. When God rules, He rules according to limited regulations so as to allow maximum freedom. But when governments rule illegitimately, they restrict freedom and increase unrighteous civil controls.

That's why whether there are Democrats or Republicans in office, right or left, there are ongoing issues on overreach and rules. It may be that there are too many laws and rules and taxes, or it may be that there are simply the wrong rules because they don't align with God's Word. God says that He is the One to set the boundary and if a nation or its people choose not to allow Him to set the boundaries, the negative results of that choice will run rampant throughout a compromised culture.

In God's kingdom agenda and according to His kingdom principles, civil government is not the only government. There also exists self-government and family government. There is ecclesiastical government as well, which functions in the church. None of these governments ought to illegitimately impose themselves on or over the others.

It doesn't take a genius to see that this illegitimate imposing of rule and reach has happened in our world. It also doesn't take a genius to recognize the resultant issues at hand. What we have today are people who lean on their own understanding and then we wonder why the culture is a mess. It is because we no longer have a Ruler, or a divine standard, which exists outside of ourselves to which we must look and align (Isa. 65:1–2). We no longer have a perfect guide who is directing and informing our decision-making. Without the correct standard, we will fall.

What would you think of a pilot who said, "I think this is the button I should push"? Or a doctor who said, "I think this is the place I should cut"? Or a pharmacist who guesses when he or she fills your prescription bottle. Your confidence would fall flat in all these situations because you don't want someone guessing when the true, effective standard has been set.

But what do we do when the life of our nation is on the line? Do we guess how to fix it? Do we look to others who are also guessing on how to fix it? Or should we look to the One who has set the true, effective standard on how a government and nation should run?

When people want to lean on their own understanding over God's truth, it leads to racial, cultural, class, and political chaos. One of the passages that would have put an end to American slavery before it ever began was Exodus 21:16, which says if a person kidnaps another human being in order to sell them, that person has committed a capital crime worthy of death. That established standard by God would have shut down slavery right then at the start. But people skipped it in order not to follow through on the freedom God has offered to all. Even people in the church skipped God's standard in order to justify the creation and maintenance of an economic system based on pure evil and greed.

God has established government and how it is to run. When people and politicians turn from His standard of government, the consequences are great. We see this in what happened to Adam. He chose to eat from the Google Tree in his den. He took the one thing he was instructed to leave alone. As a result, God carried out the consequence He had let Adam know he would get. Genesis 2:17 made it clear that Adam was free to make his own choices and had an abundance to choose from, "but from the tree of the knowledge of good and evil you shall not eat, for in the day that you eat from it you will surely die."

Civil government is to allow maximum freedom of the good things God has provided in order for people to have the opportunity to exercise personal responsibility. It does this through the enactment of limited regulations coupled with dire consequences. Adam and Eve both suffered gravely for their wrong and disobedient choice. What's more, their family suffered. Their legacy suffered. And all of humanity has suffered and continues to suffer.

As we read earlier, Romans 13:4 declares of government, "For it is a minister of God to you for good. But if you do what is evil, be afraid; for it does not bear the sword for nothing; for it is a minister of God, an avenger who brings wrath on the one who practices evil." The government that governs according to God's righteous and just principles is to serve as an instrument of intimidation and judgment against evil. The reason is because mankind is sinful and unless there are consequences for the sins and the evils in the world, they will be left unchecked. Every parent knows that in order to control and manage the activity in the home there must be consequences tied to choices. Whether those consequences involve a limited amount of play time, or the removal of a favorite game, or whatever reasonable option a parent chooses, the consequences are there to encourage good behavior and limit the wrongdoing. In this way, children and all members in the home are better able to enjoy freedom, peace, and personal productivity.

When Adam and Eve decided to choose wrongly, they lost the freedom of enjoying a happy home. Instead, they ushered in conflict with one another and with their sons. They also lost the freedom of enjoying their work because now God said they would "toil" in their work. They lost the freedom of enjoying a healthy environment because now they worked in a land where only "thorns and thistles" would grow. The whole reason they went from paradise to personal prisons of pain is because they settled for Satan's lies. They got tricked by the devil who told them they didn't really need God anyhow. He smooth-talked them into thinking they could make their own choices based on their own knowledge of good and evil if they would just eat from the forbidden fruit. By setting their own rules, they lost their freedom. When people reject God, they invite tyranny. And when people invite tyranny, they lose freedom. And when people lose freedom, they live in bondage. On the other hand, when people are released to experience and enjoy the freedom that God offers within His established boundaries, they are simultaneously released to serve and seek the well-being of others (Gal. 5:13). As Nelson Mandela said, "For to be free is not merely to cast off one's chains, but to live in a way that respects and enhances the freedom of others."[3]

God defines the healthy running of a civil government as one that maximizes freedom, offers limited regulations, but also attaches significant consequences when those regulations are broken. When that is done and supported by politicians and civilians alike, the nation will truly be known as the home of the free. We will then be able to let freedom ring and exclaim the refrain together, "Free at last! free at last! Thank God Almighty, we are free at last."[4]

3. Nelson Mandela, *Long Walk to Freedom* (New York: Back Bay Books, 1995), 655.
4. Martin Luther King Jr., "I Have a Dream," address delivered at the March on Washington for Jobs and Freedom, August 28, 1963. Transcript at *The Avalon Project*, Yale Law School, 2008, avalon.law.yale.edu/20th_century/mlk01.asp.

Chapter 4

THE PILLARS OF RIGHTEOUSNESS AND JUSTICE

September 11 will be a day that will live in infamy in the history of the United States of America. It was on this day in 2001 that the United States was attacked by another kingdom. A foreign kingdom invaded our land, bringing destruction through the devastating demise of the Twin Towers in New York City. When those two towers came down, the entire nation was turned upside down and everything changed. From that day forward, our nation viewed its enemies differently, especially with regard to how we would fight. Our nation established laws differently regarding how each of us would travel, and set up security measures differently so that we would never again be invaded by a foreign kingdom in that way.

The Twin Towers were targeted for many reasons. One of the reasons was most likely because they represented something that stood for the well-being of our citizenry. When it comes to God's governance of the universe, He has His own twin towers, or pillars, of His kingdom rule over His creation. These two towers stand tall. To the degree that these towers are left unattacked by foreign philosophies, worldviews, and foreign kingdoms, the government of our nation—and the government of any nation who honors these two towers—stands tall.

Yet when these twin towers are misused, disregarded, mishandled, or even destroyed, the nation cannot stand. In Psalm 89:11, we see that both the heavens and the earth belong to God. God is in charge of it all. He created both so He rules over both. But looking further at this passage, we also discover how He rules over both. We read:

> The heavens are Yours, the earth also is Yours;
> The world and all it contains, You have founded them.
> The north and the south, You have created them;
> Tabor and Hermon shout for joy at Your name.
> You have a strong arm;
> Your hand is mighty, Your right hand is exalted.
> Righteousness and justice are the foundation of Your throne;
> Lovingkindness and truth go before You. (vv. 11–14)

The twin towers and pillars of God's kingdom are righteousness and justice. These two concepts are married like a husband and wife. They are inseparable. To the degree that a government establishes and operates by righteousness and justice as God defines them, they will succeed. These twins must be knit together and never separated if a government is to operate based on God's rule. The Bible is clear that God's throne (i.e., His kingdom) runs this way. The casual reading of Scripture clearly demonstrates how often these two concepts are intimately connected. (For example, see Deut. 32:4; Job 37:23; Ps. 33:5; 97:2; 99:4; Isa. 51:5; 56:1; 28:17; 32:16; 33:5; 56:1; Amos 5:24; Rom. 3:26.)

The closer our government is to God's government, the more ordered society will be. The further our government is from God's prescribed method of ruling according to both righteousness and justice, the more chaotic the culture will become, since it rejected God's priority for how civil government should operate. God alone is the final standard for determining what is good and what is evil.

The basis of both righteousness and justice has to do with law. We establish laws to establish righteousness and justice in society. God has already declared, as we saw in James 4:12, that He is the lawgiver. Romans 13:1 also states that every ordinance belongs to Him. That makes the first question, when it comes to righteousness and justice, to discover what God says about both. Because once you deviate from Him, you are messing with the twin towers. When either or both of these towers begin to fall, so does civilization, culture, and order.

Keep in mind, the biblical role of government is to maintain a safe, just, righteous, and compassionately responsible environment for freedom to flourish. Every Christian is to function as a kingdom independent, which means there is no ultimate loyalty to one earthly party over another. The reason for this is there is only One lawgiver, and all laws should reflect His government. No one party fully represents God's rule of righteousness and justice.

Righteousness is *the standard of right and wrong that has been established by God*. It is right because He says it is right. Or it is wrong because He says it is wrong. Things are not right because you think they are right, or because the culture, media, educational institutions, or Hollywood says they are right. That is merely human opinion. The fact that we look to human opinions to inform our standards and values, rather than divine law and ordinances, means that we have created for ourselves a competing god. God does not like competition. He calls it idolatry.

Every human law is to be a manifestation and reflection of divine law (Ezra 7:25–26). It is to mirror His law. Our laws established by our government ought to seek to mirror God's laws to the highest degree possible. That's why God told the kings to study His laws.

They were instructed to find out what He had to say about how they should rule. These kings were to pass human laws based on divinely established laws. In this manner, what God calls right or wrong would be the measure of what should then be established in the land.

From the beginning of history, it has been Satan's goal to switch the rules. This is like switching tags on clothing in a store. Satan places a different value on things than God does. What God values highly, Satan labels as cheap. What God says is cheap, Satan labels as expensive and valuable. Satan has set out to give rulers, cultures, and individuals values they were never meant to have. When humanity follows in step, it creates chaos in society and in civil government.

What Satan told Eve was that if she would just take a bite of the fruit, she would be able to determine good and evil for herself. As you know, Eve ate. And what we have today is people seeking to create their own standards of what is right and what is wrong based on what they think or how they feel. As a result, mankind has enacted a lower standard than God's and invited chaos into the culture.

The Bible says that God's Word is the perfect law (James 1:25). It has no flaws in it. God makes no mistakes. You cannot have a righteous society apart from following His law and aligning with it. The only way to maintain a just and righteous nation is for the laws and ordinances of the land to be established according to God's standards. This reminds me of my son Jonathan who came to show me how he could dunk the basketball when he was only eleven years old. Jonathan took me to the gym and proceeded to demonstrate how he had learned to dunk.

He did dunk the ball. But he also had someone else lower the standard. The janitor had taken the rim from ten feet high and dropped it down to six feet. Jonathan was trying to impress me by lowering the standard in order to accomplish the goal. But when I told the janitor to raise the rim back up to where it belonged, Jonathan could no longer dunk the ball. I looked at him and told him,

"Your goal is not to lower the standard in order to impress people. Your goal is to keep the standard where it belongs and then you grow and work diligently to raise it."

What we need in our government and in our politics is a commitment to operate on the divine standard God has established. We need to raise up citizens, led by kingdom disciples, who are willing and able to function at that standard. What we have done, however, is lower the standard so that everyone gets a prize. So everyone can feel like they've arrived. But what we have created is a society of low standards, which is crumbling before our eyes.

The Bible tells us that righteousness is the foundation of justice (Deut. 32:3–4). Just like the engine in a car needs fuel in order for it to function as it was designed to, a nation needs righteousness in order for it to operate at the optimal level it was designed for. Proverbs 14:34 tells us that, "Righteousness exalts a nation, but sin is a disgrace to *any* people." And again, righteousness builds the city, wickedness tears it down (Prov. 11:11). A nation grows in productivity, power, and progress when righteousness reigns. Yet the rampant spread and even endorsement of evil pulls a nation down to a level of utter disgrace.

If a nation enacts and abides by what God says is right, the whole nation will benefit. When it chooses to go against what God says, we read the results in Romans 1:18. It says, "For the wrath of God is revealed from heaven against all ungodliness and unrighteousness of men who suppress the truth in unrighteousness."

When a nation and her leaders choose to embrace unrighteousness, God's judgment is poured out against it. Now, that judgment won't show up as "fire and brimstone" in the church age in which we live. Rather, God says He turns a nation or individuals "over" to their own evil propensities (Rom. 1:24–28). Within these evil propensities and actions are the built-in consequences of God's wrath that result from divine abandonment.

God releases the nation to a life without Him. He lets the nation and its citizens see what life looks like without Him. In other words, when laws are passed that justify unrighteous activity and legalize evil, such as abortion, same-sex marriage, gerrymandering, redlining, etc. regarding how human beings are treated or valued, then the nation has invited God's judgment. The nation has asked for chaos to ensue.

This cause-and-effect scenario is easy to understand when it comes to certain laws like gravity. The law of gravity simply states that what goes up must come down. It's just the way things work. But let's say a person doesn't like that law. Let's look at what happens if someone doesn't really feel that the law of gravity is the way things should be. This person would rather make up their own mind about going up or down. So the person decides to climb a building and step off the rooftop into thin air. What do you think happens to that person and his or her belief in gravity?

The consequences of their ill-informed choice will consume them and take their life when they hit the pavement. The law of gravity is a law that comes with real consequences. You cannot defy it. You cannot rebel against it and survive. Gravity could care less how you feel or what you believe. When you buck it, you do so to your own devastation.

When a nation on any level bucks right and wrong behaviors as God calls them to be, it gets swept up off the pavement of history. When a nation rebels against the laws of God, it receives for itself and its inhabitants the just results of its choices and actions. God is near to the nation who follows His rule, but He is far from the nation that does not (Deut. 4:7–8). Putting "In God We Trust" on our money or declaring that we are "one nation under God" is not enough when unrighteousness is the standard by which a nation is defined or governed. God will disconnect Himself from any nation that exalts false gods rather than Him. Keep in mind, an idol or a false god does not need to be referred to as a "god"—it just needs to shape and influence our decision-making more than God. The religion of humanism and the idolatry of man has invited God's passive wrath of divine abandonment into the land, and Christians have been co-conspirators in this regard.

Righteousness as God defines it must be the standard. But correlating with righteousness comes justice. While righteousness is the standard of right and wrong, justice is *the impartial and equitable application of God's moral law in society.* It's possible to have righteous laws without a just application of those laws. The laws on the books may be right but the people executing and enforcing the laws may be wrong. A nation needs right laws, but it also needs the just application of those laws in order for society to work. Justice refers to enacting the right way. It is righteousness applied impartially in society.

You wouldn't want your doctor to write a prescription only to have your pharmacist fill it with the wrong medication. The law from the doctor may be right but when it is enacted the wrong way at the pharmacy, you will be messed up. You cannot have righteousness without justice if it is going to work in society.

Justice is the standard that privileges and penalties are distributed in society. Proverbs 8:15 puts it like this, "By me kings reign, and rulers decree justice." It is by God that any political leader is to reign, whether it is the president, Congress, or legislators. They are not to leave God out. That's why it is an insult when Christians leave out God's standard of right and wrong from their own conversations or debates. It is also an insult when Christians fail to apply God's righteous and just standards to their own lives and relationships.

The Bible declares that there is no injustice with God (Deut. 32:4). He is a just God and He demands just application of His rules. However, we tend to do what Mark 7:8–9 says, by nullifying the Word of God with the traditions of men.

We enact cancel culture on God when we lift what people or politicians think above what He says. The first question any believer should ask on any matter is, What does God have to say about it? We must examine what God thinks and what He has expressed on each and every issue. The Bible tells us that it is the wicked rulers who decree unjust laws, particularly for the poor and the oppressed (Isa. 10:1–2). When we recognize politicians or policies producing outcomes of oppression, even if they are posited as a policy that is good, we must hold them to account against God's standards of righteousness and justice. We must not support that which seeks to exploit the vulnerable and needy.

Man's justice should reflect God's justice (Deut. 1:17). It's not about calling all things fair. It is about looking at the way God details biblical justice and then living according to His rules. Leviticus 19:15 puts it like this, "You shall do no injustice in judgment; you shall not be partial to the poor nor defer to the great, but you are to judge your neighbor fairly." We are not to have one standard for the rich and another standard for the poor.

God's justice must be equitable across the board. He doesn't play favorites. You are not to use your position, power, or economic status to buy your way out of justice, which is what we witness to a large degree in our culture today. Someone who is rich will get sentenced for a certain amount of drugs in one way while someone who is poor is sentenced another way. The law is the same but the application of justice with regard to the law, far too often, is not.

When we allow people with power and clout to skirt around the law while the poor and needy feel the full brunt of it, that is not an equal representation of justice. This area of justice and injustice must be addressed by the church. Rulers must be respectfully confronted with God's standards and then apply them consistently across the board. God speaks on economic justice, criminal justice, social justice, environmental justice, and all manner of conflicts in His Word. He has left nothing out.

For example, when it comes to the area of criminal justice, God declares in Scripture that a person cannot be condemned by one witness. Deuteronomy 17:6 says there must be corroborating evidence. In fact, He goes on to say that if a witness comes and lies because they are trying to get someone in trouble, this witness then must bear the penalty that the other party would have borne if found guilty (Deut. 19:18–19). That would change a lot in the courtrooms today. If a person were found guilty of perjury and placed under the same penalty of the defendant had the defendant been found guilty, we would have a lot more truth-telling on the witness stand than we do now.

God has addressed the issues we face in society throughout His Word. He addressed slavery in Exodus 21:16 where we read, "He who kidnaps a man, whether he sells him or he is found in his possession, shall surely be put to death." Talk about solving a problem before it even begins. As I noted earlier, the just application of this one law would have solved the issue of slavery overnight. But ministers failed to preach the whole council of God. Congregants failed to read the whole council of God. Thus, politicians failed to enact the whole council of God.

When the church fails to speak out on comprehensive justice, society suffers. If the church were dealing with this one area rightly and justly, slavery would not have taken root as deeply or as long as it did. But because the church was more concerned with growing its own pocketbook as well as cultural acceptance through the unjust gains of slavery amongst its members, we are now a nation judged by God for this evil, and much more.

God cares for the oppressed and the vulnerable. We often hear preachers speak on the destruction of Sodom and Gomorrah and how it was destroyed due to moral decay in the areas of homosexuality. But far too often, what is left out is what we read in Ezekiel 16:49. This is where we see God's heart and why He brought about such a swift and terrible end to this group of people and their cities. We read, "Behold, this was the guilt of your sister Sodom: she and her daughters had arrogance, abundant food and careless ease, but she did not help the poor and needy."

Sodom and Gomorrah were destroyed because of social injustice in the oppression of the weak and the poor. God will destroy a nation not only for its unrighteousness but also for its injustice. By the way, the Civil War was allowed by God. Civil war took place in the United States because God got tired of the injustice being done to the black population in our land. Since the church wasn't willing to stand up and rectify things, God allowed a war to break out which cut short the lives and legacies of many people. The Civil War was theological and spiritual, not just social and political. But if you do not understand how God works and how He pours out His wrath on a nation against injustice, then you will not recognize the issues we face today in our country and culture as spiritual in nature.

The issues we struggle with today have been allowed by God in part because of the injustice that has gone on unaddressed. Whether it is due to racism, classism, elitism, or infanticide and abortion, God allows chaos into a culture when righteousness and justice are absent. In fact, the Bible says that if there is no justice, you don't even have to bother to worship (Amos 5:21–24). Micah 6:8 makes it clear what we are to be about as people of God: "He has told you, O man, what is good; and what does the LORD require of you but to do justice, to love kindness, and to walk humbly with your God?"

God demands righteousness and justice if a society is going to function properly. This is why the jubilee principle is so powerful. It's a principle found in Luke 4 that Jesus laid out when He launched His public ministry. Jesus presented an alternative to how society was currently operating. In the temple, He stood up and quoted Isaiah 18 to begin. We read in Luke 4,

And He came to Nazareth, where He had been brought up; and as was His custom, He entered the synagogue on the Sabbath, and stood up to read. And the book of the prophet Isaiah was handed to Him. And He opened the book and found the place where it was written,

"The Spirit of the Lord is upon Me,
Because He anointed Me to preach the gospel to the poor.
He has sent Me to proclaim release to the captives,
And recovery of sight to the blind,
To set free those who are oppressed,
To proclaim the favorable year of the Lord."

And He closed the book, gave it back to the attendant and
sat down; and the eyes of all in the synagogue were fixed on
Him. And He began to say to them, "Today this Scripture
has been fulfilled in your hearing." (vv. 16–21)

Jesus stood up and in reading this passage He proclaimed the
favorable year of the Lord. This is a reference to the year of jubilee.
Jesus took His audience all the way back to Leviticus 25 where the
principle initially was stated. The year of jubilee is when God restruc-
tured society to function righteously and justly. It took place every
forty-ninth year, because by then humanity had allowed things to get
out of order. Not only would things be out of order from a standpoint
of economic oppression, but it would be out of order from a standpoint of land use and ownership. Governments were overextended,
and many people were oppressed, economically enslaved, or in need.
In this forty-ninth year, God would fix things through what was called
the year of jubilee. *Jubilee* meant "celebration of good news." The good
news was that the mess of injustice would be addressed, wrongs would
be righted, and order would be restored in society.

It is at this time that the oppressed would be set free. The illegitimately incarcerated would be released. The slaves would no longer
be slaves. A jubilee was granted in order to re-establish equity in the
land. We need a jubilee in our land today as well. But we won't get a
jubilee from Congress. We won't get a jubilee from our president. We

won't get a jubilee from our judges. In order to inaugurate a jubilee, it has to come from God. The spiritual must always precede the social.

What's more, the jubilee always and only starts when attached to the Day of Atonement. Leviticus 25 goes into the details of this day, but essentially it entails coming right before God in humility under His approved sacrifice for our sins, which in the church age is Jesus Christ. Until we, as believers, humble ourselves before Jesus Christ and accept His atonement for our sins collectively and choose to honor Him as Lord, the collective church cannot usher in the jubilee.

Please note that the opportunity for jubilee is called "good news." This refers to the scope of the gospel. While the content of the gospel is narrow, referring to the death and resurrection of Christ for the forgiveness of sins and the gift of eternal life—the scope of the gospel is broad, referring to the social and political effects of the gospel's impact in society. Thus, justice is a part of the scope of the gospel. The content of the gospel points you to heaven, while the scope of the gospel brings heaven's standards into history. Christians must be committed to evangelism and justice.

The thing that helped the civil rights movement to accomplish all that it did was the church showing up to confess the sins of slavery, racism, and pride together. The church marched and went public on this issue. Now, I'm not saying every single church did that or every single church member did, but a tipping point occurred when a certain number did.

When a percentage of the church got right and unified on this issue, unrighteous laws were challenged and changed in our land. That's why you'll always hear me say that it is not as important who we have in the White House, it is much more important how we are functioning in the church house. If God can get His folk in the pews to be righteous and just, as well as to stand up for righteousness and justice, He will then let that overflow like streams of water into the land. He will not start with politics or politicians and then work backward to His church. Cultural change for good starts with the church and her members.

The Bible speaks to all the issues we are wrestling with today and it is up to us as representatives of the King and His kingdom to reflect them and inject them into society. For example, the Bible also speaks to righteousness and justice as it relates to the issue of immigration. When looking at immigration from a spiritual perspective, you'll quickly see that one primary goal of immigration for Christians is evangelism and discipleship. Scripture is clear that immigrants are to be treated with kindness and love (Ex. 22:21; 23:9; Lev. 19:33–34; Deut. 10:19). This opens the door for the presentation of the gospel to those who do not yet know Christ as Lord. God's goal is that all nations would serve Him (Ps. 72:8–11). Thus, the goal of Christians is always first and foremost to seek to proclaim Christ to all.

Kindness and love must be extended even through how governments look at immigration. Since governments are to operate under biblical standards that provide for the safety, security, and well-being of its citizens for good (Rom. 13:1–7; 1 Peter 2:13–14), then immigration policies must be legal and beneficial to the country and its citizens. This can only be done through a controlled immigration process to assure immigrants are advancing the well-being and progress of the nation and are not detrimental to it. When immigration is conducted in that manner, all people benefit. When it is not and illegal immigration is allowed to flourish, consequences occur.

Two sins have been committed regarding illegal immigrants that are already in America. First, they broke the law by how they entered the country. Secondly, the country has utilized these immigrants through work exploitation to help build the economy. When two competing sins have been committed, the solution is what decision will glorify God the most. This is demonstrated in Scripture by the honoring of midwives who lied to Pharaoh about the birth of the Hebrew children (Ex. 1:15–21). It was also demonstrated by God honoring Rahab who lied about not knowing where the Hebrew spies were (Josh. 2:1–21). God honored both because when faced with two choices, death vs. lying, their choice brought God the greatest glory. Therefore, in the case of immigration that has been initiated unlawfully and also reinforced through unlawful exploitation of workers and wages, protecting the unity and primacy of the nuclear family of the immigrant families, as well as valuing their contribution to our economy, should allow them to stay under the following conditions:

1. All illegal immigrants are required to register themselves and their nuclear family members within a specified time, or they will be immediately deported.
2. They will then have access to services the United States offers along with a worker's permit that will allow them to be productive residents and paid more fairly.
3. A stringent path to citizenship should be offered that involves time, a fine, and no felony convictions. This should also include the requirement to learn the English language, demonstrating gainful employment, and payment of taxes.

These conditions should be accomplished by a strict legal border immigration policy that controls all entrances into the country, vets all applicants, and immediately removes all felons. Entering the nation illegally is wrong; however, it is just as wrong for the citizens of the nation to exploit illegal immigrants through unfair wages and a lack of care.

When you have injustice in the systems seeking to fix injustice in the systems, you aren't going to get very far. It is the body of Christ who is to stand up and look for ways to serve the underserved, or release those from oppression. We ought to aggressively seek out how to remove redlining and gerrymandering that has kept people from being able to take advantage of goods and land readily available to countless others. We need to address areas where voter suppression has kept people from quick and easy access to voice their beliefs in a vote. We need to go above and beyond what is required to do justice and show kindness in the land. Oppression and injustice must be rectified and there is no better place to start to address it than with those who claim the name of Christ and seek to uphold His law of love in their lives.

It is time for God's people to lead the way in making sure our laws are righteous and just. We can do this by electing and supporting those politicians who support righteous policies. But it is also time for God's people to lead the way in making sure that our righteous laws are carried out in a just way. We can do this through what we say, post, support, and engage in as well as electing those politicians who promote a kingdom worldview throughout the nation. Where there is injustice, we must address it. But we must also be willing to forgive those who brought it about when they repent.

When Jesus hung on the cross, He understood firsthand what it was like to not be able to breathe. He labored for every breath He took until He eventually succumbed to death itself. Yet as He could barely breathe, He asked God the Father to forgive those who were oppressing Him. Jesus knew the power and need for forgiveness. When we say, "No justice, no peace," we need to also say, "No forgiveness, no peace." We need healing in our land on all levels and in all people. May the example of Jesus Christ usher in order in our society, and may His example be manifested first and foremost by His church.

PART TWO

The Concerns of Kingdom Politics

Chapter 5

THE SANCTITY OF LIFE

If you go and buy a box of checkers, you'll notice something on each piece. On one side of every playing piece is a crown. This is because the piece has been designed with a purpose. That purpose is to get the piece to the end of the board in order to receive kingship.

Yet while the checker pieces were created to reach a destiny of royalty, there exists an abortion process in this game. Each player on opposing sides makes it his or her goal to block and abort the other side from reaching royalty status. If they jump an opponent's piece, the piece is removed altogether. Some of the aborting of the checkers occurs early in the game. Other times, it happens late in the game. Yet whether it happens early or late, the end result is the same. Without reaching the other side, the checker piece has not fulfilled its greatest potential.

In exploring the area of kingdom politics, we must look at the partnership with God that Christians have been allowed and encouraged to join in regard to expanding His rule in society through civil government. When we recognize that civil government is the role of the established government to reflect and maintain a safe, just, and righteously compassionate environment for freedom to flourish, we cannot escape the importance of examining government's relationship to life itself. At the core of the establishment of government is the safety and well-being of its citizens. Government does not bear the sword in vain. It is to use its power to get rid of evil while promoting good in order to allow individuals the opportunity to maximize their own destinies in this game of life.

God is the creator of life. Therefore, in any discussion on government and life, we must start with God. When God created humanity in Genesis 1:26–28, He said that He wanted to create mankind in His own image. Thus, any discussion of life in any human form starts with the *imago Dei*—the image of God. If you fail to start with the image of God, you make life into something you define rather than recognizing it by what God has created it to be.

The psalmist describes God's view of humanity to us in Psalm 8:4–6, "What is man that You take thought of him, and the son of man that You care for him? Yet You have made him a little lower than God, and You crown him with glory and majesty! You make him to rule over the works of Your hands; You have put all things under his feet." Human beings are majestic in creation. We are a spectacular masterpiece in the hand of God Himself. What makes each of us so majestic is that we have on us the mark of God. We have been stamped from the beginning with the image of God Himself.

This means that every human being has a divine design. Every human being is sacred. Every person is designed to reflect God's heart and His image, which also means that we were all created for community. God is not an isolated being. He exists as a triune Being— one God who is composed of three co-equal Persons who are one in essence but distinct in personality. We, as human beings created in His image, were also created for one another. Every person matters. Every individual is significant. Every life counts.

You will often hear somebody say the phrase, "You remind me of somebody." Perhaps you've said it yourself. But guess what God did when He created mankind? He created a race of beings to exist as divine reminders of Himself. Every life enters this world full of dignity, splendor, uniqueness, and glory.

Now, granted, like a broken mirror, our humanity has been damaged. We were created to reflect God and to represent Him in all of life, but our reflection has been broken through the introduction of sin. The enemy on the other side of the checkerboard has sought to discover ways to abort our advancement in life. Satan has sought to distort the image of our divine royalty through introducing evil into this world. If you take a cursory glance at culture, you can see that he has been successful in many ways.

One of the ways he has been successful is through the destruction of life itself so that there is no chance of advancing at all. The Bible is clear that we should not murder (Ex. 20:13). Whether it's homicide, suicide, patricide, genocide, matricide, fratricide, or infanticide—whenever a life is taken, it becomes an attack on God Himself. This is why we read in Genesis 9:6, "Whoever sheds man's blood, by man his blood shall be shed, for in the image of God He made man." Life is so precious to God that the only way to pay for illegitimately taking the life of another is to forfeit your own.

Civil government should be legislating life, not death.

God views the taking of life as a personal insult. As a result, He set out to establish clear boundaries against the removal of anyone's life by the hands of another. Any discussion of life has to start with the divine mark and standard of life God has established. The job of the government is to protect life. That's why safety is often considered one of the first responsibilities of a government. Yet when a nation leaves God out of government, thus allowing life and its value to be downgraded, reduced, dishonored, and attacked, the nation itself will crumble from within.

Civil government should be legislating life, not death. Especially since babies' heartbeats can be detected as early as six weeks. When you buy a picture frame, it comes with a generic photo inside of someone you do not know, so you discard it. This is because you are going to put another picture inside of yourself, family, or friends. Then you hang it up or put it on display. The generic picture has no value, but the personal picture has special value. A baby in the frame of the womb of its mother is not a lifeless reality to be discarded but rather a life that is to be valued, treasured, and held in high esteem.

When you and I think about kingdom politics and our role within it, we must think about life. We must consider the safety and well-being of all life—whether this life is in the womb or not. Because just like in the game of checkers, some pieces can be aborted early on, or some pieces can be aborted further into the game—yet any removal of that piece is an abortion of the forward progress to its destiny.

A WHOLE-LIFE AGENDA

One of the problems that arises when it comes to evaluating politics in our land is that we often key in on a term of life, rather than the whole of life. We choose to focus on the preborn life, but disregard the life outside of the womb. Or, on the other side of the aisle, we look at the life outside of the womb while disregarding the rights of the life in the womb. Yet if we are to view life according to God's standards, we must view all of life as sacred.

An often-used Scripture to emphasize the value of life in the womb similarly emphasizes the value of life after being born. However, we skip over the reality of the latter part far too often. Let's take a look at the Scripture in its entirety:

For You formed my inward parts;
You wove me in my mother's womb.
I will give thanks to You, for I am fearfully and wonderfully
   made;
Wonderful are Your works, and my soul knows it very well.
My frame was not hidden from You,
When I was made in secret,
And skillfully wrought in the depths of the earth;
Your eyes have seen my unformed substance;
And in Your book were all written
The days that were ordained for me,
When as yet there was not one of them. (Ps. 139:13–16)

This passage reveals God's recognition of and care for life within the womb, and it also reveals to us God's plan for life outside of the womb. The reason why God's care existed from the beginning is because He had "days that were ordained" for each of us. He has a plan for us. God's value of life isn't only focused on life in the womb. The creative genius of God views all of life as sacred.

Abortion should be a major issue as Christians navigate politics today. God has spoken on the issue of abortion. In Job 10:8–12 as well as Job 31:5, we read that God has made each individual in the womb. We have the qualities of God in our unborn state. Psalm 22:9–10 refer to the baby in the womb as someone whom God takes particular interest in and provides care for in order to bring to delivery. Similarly, in Matthew 1:20, when Mary was pregnant with the Lord Jesus Christ, the angel told Joseph that Mary was carrying a child. She was not carrying a "glob" of something. She didn't have a non-person within her. Mary was carrying a baby. She was with child, and God brings the child out of the womb (Ps. 22:9–10).

The Bible is clear that life resides in the womb. The Bible is also clear that God is so committed to life in the womb that He prescribes its value before this life ever gets into the womb. We read this in Isaiah 49:5 where it says, "And now says the LORD, who formed Me from the womb to be His Servant."

Also in Jeremiah 1:4–5 it says, "Now the word of the LORD came to me saying, 'Before I formed you in the womb I knew you, and before you were born I consecrated you; I have appointed you a prophet to the nations.'" Numerous examples exist in Scripture to validate the truth that God places a baby in the womb because He has a plan for this life to experience his or her destiny outside of the womb. Whenever someone cuts this life short, he or she has interfered with the program and purposes of Almighty God. In fact, Matthew 1:20 reveals to us that life begins at conception (see also Galatians 1:15–16). The issue with abortion is not first whether or not a woman is going to have a child but rather whether she is going to deliver that child dead or alive.

Thus, when the government decrees that it is okay to perform an abortion, you and I must stand against this. We must speak up for the rights of the unborn who cannot speak for themselves. When we don't and this form of homicide is allowed to continue, then we can expect the consequences in culture. Scripture says that when innocent blood is shed, more blood will be shed (Ps. 106:36–40; Prov. 6:17; Joel 3:19). The fact that the fetus is in a perpetual state of growth and that a heartbeat can be detected as early as six weeks proves it is a life to be protected, not destroyed. We can expect crime rates to go up. We can expect conflict to increase. Whenever we allow and condone the attack of life made in the image of God, especially innocent life, God unleashes His vengeance on the culture that allows it. Legislating and legalizing death in the womb opens a Pandora's box of criminal activity as a spiritual repercussion in society itself. Every individual has been created with a recognition of their divinely ordained dignity from conception.

As a pastor, I've heard my fair share of arguments for abortion by those wishing to get one. The main argument being that it is a woman's body to do with as she chooses. This argument always causes me great confusion because anyone knows that if a woman is carrying a male child, then there are obvious parts within her body that do not belong to her. You cannot equate a life within a body as the body itself. Secondly, Scripture has solemnly declared that life is the creation of God and made in the image of God. Just because this life comes housed within another life while he or she is developing does not mean you get to do whatever you want with him or her, especially since the destiny of the unborn child is different than that of the mother.

In fact, the government makes laws all the time that negate allowing people to do whatever they want with their bodies. If you choose to drink to the point of being drunk and then go out and drive, you will be violating the law. Even though it is your own body that consumed the alcohol and then drove. There are boundaries on freedom that are established in order to protect the rights and freedoms of others as well. A drunk person cannot argue that it's his or her body so therefore they have the right to drive however they want to. Neither can a rapist argue that he is using his own body to rape someone else. There are laws against the use of our own bodies if that use infringes upon the rights, freedom, and safety of others. We should only establish laws against doing wrong, including sex with minors, incest, murder—and the same should be true for the life of the unborn through abortion.

In addition, the baby in the womb is an entirely different genetic code than the mother carrying the child. It cannot be scientifically argued that it is her body because the DNA of the baby is not the DNA of the mom. Abortion has nothing to do with a woman's right to her own body. It has everything to do with the selfishness of our world, which has reduced and dumbed down the dignity of life in order to justify the taking of it at will.

My assistant, Sylvia, has a very intriguing story. She tells her story publicly and so I am telling it by permission. As a teenager, Sylvia was raped. As a result of the rape, she got pregnant. Because of the trauma of the rape, Sylvia decided to get an abortion. But something went awry when she went to get the abortion and she wound up changing her mind. Subsequently, Sylvia committed her life to Jesus Christ and later became a part of our church's ministry. She began to raise her son, the son of a rape victim, and they both grew in the Lord together. As her son continued to grow, he wanted to be used by God. He later went on to lead a whole region of Campus Impact in order to give young people a spiritual perspective on life.

God had a divine design on this man's life, and he was allowed to accomplish it because of Sylvia's willingness to honor the life within her womb. Even though she has been my assistant for nearly four decades now and has been blessed with a marriage to a godly man for several decades as well, the reality of her choice still impacts her. She recently came to me with tears in her eyes and said, "Pastor, all I can do is cry because I thought I was going to abort my baby, but I let him live and now, to see him serving the Lord and impacting a generation of young people as well as to see my grandsons following in his footsteps brings tears of gratitude to my eyes."

Had Sylvia gone through with the abortion, it would have cut off the destiny of her son, but it would have also cut off the destiny of her grandsons. Yet because she came to understand that God is the author of life and the sustainer of those who trust in Him, she has seen Him do wonders for her own life, healing, and legacy. We must realize that abortion cancels the only life on earth that a child could ever have. When we make God's standard our standard, He allows us to see the blessing of His power and protection.

Kingdom politics insists that Christians should righteously and peacefully protest legislation that legalizes the arbitrary taking of the lives of the unborn. The exception to this is when the health and life of the mother is at stake. Otherwise, adoption should be the preferred option for those who choose not to keep the child to raise. Of course, men should be held legally and strictly accountable to provide for the children they sire. Life should be guarded and nourished in the womb. Kingdom politics reflects that stand. But here's where we often run into problems. We will frequently find Christians on the side of politics that seeks to protect life in the womb, but oftentimes they will then disregard life to the tomb.

There must be laws to protect the existence of life. But there also must be laws to protect the dignity of life as well. American slavery, for example, was a legal institution that stripped slaves of their dignity. Criminal leasing stripped many people, particularly men, of their dignity. Jim Crow laws removed dignity from an entire group of people. Racism, in any form, results in a loss of dignity. Whether racism exists for individuals, families, or structurally, it cancels out the dignity of those oppressed. It removes the crown that exists on every man and woman born into this world. Putting your knee on the neck of a helpless victim not only destroys his life, but it is also an attack on his dignity.

That's why the Bible says in James 3:9 that we are not to reduce the dignity of another through cursing. Each person is made in the image of God. When you remove a person's dignity from them by telling them the color of their skin prevents them from certain opportunities or prevents them from participating as an equal in society, you are essentially cursing the *imago Dei*. When you treat the homeless as though they have no dignity or when you treat the poor as though they were the leftovers or refuse in life, you are cursing the *imago Dei*. When governments enact structures and systems in society to reduce a certain group of people from living life to their fullest potential, these governments are cursing the *imago Dei*. No matter how torn or how tattered a wrinkled dollar bill is, it is the image on it that determines its value. A smooth dollar bill has no right to reject or reduce the value of a wrinkled one.

Whether that shows up in gerrymandering of districts or redlining of neighborhoods so that there is no equal access, or whether it shows up in the de-emphasis on education in certain areas over others—it is an afront to the image of God. When access to quality health care becomes attainable for some but not for others based on a judgment in society or a practice through political means, it is an attack on God because God values all life. Aborting the length or well-being of a person's existence is an affront to God Himself. He created each of us with a unique plan to fulfill and path to pursue, which will bring Him glory and advance His kingdom agenda on earth.

When appraisers go into appraisal districts and underbid housing so that they can have gentrification rushed in and people are not given the value of their property, that is lowering the dignity of a group of individuals for the benefit of another group. When this and a multitude of other strategies is employed either formally or informally to lift one group higher than another, these policies go against God's intended order. What's more, when Christians say nothing to reject these policies or systems, they inadvertently become co-conspirators to oppressive regimes that are aborting the dignity of God's image bearers. Just like Mordecai challenged Esther to go before the king (i.e., government) to fight for the right to life for her people both present and future (Esth. 4), Christians should appeal to civil government for the right to life for all today.

A GOD OF RIGHTEOUSNESS AND JUSTICE

Psalm 89:14 tells us that God is a God of both righteousness and justice. He doesn't uphold righteousness at the expense of justice, nor does He uphold justice at the expense of righteousness. You can't have one without the other. They stand as twin towers. They operate simultaneously. Yet when the body of Christ is split down the middle, with some on one side calling for righteousness in the protection of life in the womb, but some on the other side calling for justice in the protection of life and dignity outside of the womb—you have a

THE SANCTITY OF LIFE

house divided. It must be both. We must, as kingdom followers of Jesus Christ, call for the protection of life in the womb and to the tomb. We must not subscribe to a term-life agenda. Believers are to pursue a whole-life agenda because that is what God instructs us in His Word. He calls for a kingdom agenda for all of life.

There exist two kinds of abortion in our world today. There's abortion in the womb, but there is also abortion when people do not get to live out their divinely ordained destiny. There is no baby in the womb or life born from the womb who does not have the stamp of God on him or her. The whole political system, if it is to reflect God's kingdom politics, should be designed to enhance the ability of all life to reach his or her divinely ordained destiny. This clarion call for our culture ought to be led by Christians. And yet Christians remain so deeply divided that even obtaining a coherent conversation on the two subjects is rare these days. Every person has a right to life, but that means a right to all of life—not just the right to be born.

This subject of life is so important that God tells us in Matthew 5:21–22 that if we call someone by a hateful name, we are in jeopardy of hell's fire. We read,

> "You have heard that the ancients were told, 'You shall not commit murder' and 'Whoever commits murder shall be liable to the court.' But I say to you that everyone who is angry with his brother shall be guilty before the court; and whoever says to his brother, 'You good-for-nothing,' shall be guilty before the supreme court; and whoever says, 'You fool,' shall be guilty enough to go into the fiery hell."

Jesus did not mince His words when it came to protecting and preserving the dignity of humanity. Even if this person's humanity is reduced and their dignity removed through a verbal attack, it is enough to enact God's judgment and wrath. If you and I are going to understand politics from God's perspective, then we must understand the kind of value God places on all of life.

To participate in the political process—whether through what you say, how you vote, or who you support financially—you have to vote for life. But you have to remember that life starts at conception and goes on till death. Between the two (conception and death), there should be dignity. Between the two, there should be safety. There should also be protection so that the individual can maximize his or her freedom within God's just and righteous boundaries established for all.

To live according to the principles of kingdom politics, there should be an emphasis on setting up structures, systems, attitudes, and perspectives that enable the opportunity for personal dignity to be maintained. As Christians, we must adopt a whole-life agenda, which seeks to protect the value of all of life at every stage and every status.

Jesus understands what it is like to live a life of oppression. For those of you who have experienced something similar, look to Him and how He responded to the systems at hand. Do not take your own revenge. Jesus Christ was in a system of infanticide, because they were killing male babies, two years old and younger, when He was born (Matt. 2:16). In fact, they were trying to kill Him. Jesus also knows what it is like to be a homeless person. As He said in Matthew 8:20, "Jesus said to him, 'The foxes have holes and the birds of the air have nests, but the Son of Man has nowhere to lay His head.'" Jesus also knows what it's like to be unjustly accused. He knows what it is like for a mob to riot and seek to destroy His life (John 5:8; 7:1, 19, 25). He knows what it is like to receive an unjust death sentence. And in spite of all He faced, He retained His dignity because His identity was rooted and founded in God Himself.

In 2 Corinthians 3:18, we are told that Jesus exists so that we might be "transformed" to His image. As we grow closer to Him and seek to reflect His kingdom values in our everyday lives, including our political allegiances and support, He will give us a new image.

He will strengthen our own self-image. Jesus can turn a racist into an anti-racist. He can turn prejudice into acceptance. He can remove discrimination. He can give dignity where it has been withheld. He can offer significance and healing for those who have gone down the wrong path of abortion. He can forgive, lift up, and restore what has been lost when you and I return to Him and abide in Him.

It is in Jesus Christ that we will discover our own personal dignity and the royalty we are destined to live out. It is also in Jesus Christ that we will discover the value and worth of each other. Once we come to understand how important life is—not just life in the womb but all of life in every stage and every station—we will know how to support policies and laws that protect the dignity and sanctity of the *imago Dei* present within each of us. We will also know to oppose the policies and laws that leave the door open for oppression or the devaluation of human life in every form and stage of existence.

Chapter 6

THE FOUNDATION OF FAMILY

I'll never forget the time when Lois and I went on vacation with the kids to Disneyland. We were enjoying the sights and the sounds of the Magic Kingdom, but somewhere between Fantasyland and Tomorrowland we lost sight of our younger son, Jonathan. We couldn't find him, and as we continued to search, panic set in. Worry consumed us because our son had been disconnected from our family. Needless to say, we looked for an extended length of time in the midst of crowds of people, but we couldn't find him on our own.

After twenty minutes or so, we went to the security attendant to ask them to help us find our lost son. After a while, he was located in one of the shops. Apparently, Jonathan had been mesmerized by the toys in the shop and had remained there while we walked on. Jonathan had allowed one kingdom—the Magic Kingdom—to distract him from his family. He allowed a distraction to take over his life at a level it was never intended to. The Magic Kingdom had a role, sure. But that role was never intended to entice a young child away from his mom or dad.

In our land today, we are living with kingdoms in conflict. We are living with kingdoms who are each competing for the attention of children and youth. These competing kingdoms oftentimes seek to rip away the fabric of the family. It's not just one kingdom that seeks to dismantle the home either. We have the kingdom of entertainment. We have the kingdom of sports. We have the kingdom of social media. And, of course, we have the kingdom of politics. All these various kingdoms share a similar goal: much of what they intend to do is absorb attention through a myriad of distractions that seek to supersede and redefine the family's influence in the home.

Whoever owns the family owns the future.

The family is the target because the family is the first institution established by God that would serve as the foundation for the well-being of society and civilization. Like pouring a foundation for a building will determine the stability of what you build on it, when God established the family, He poured the foundation upon which civilization and society would stand. If and when the foundation of the family is shaken, cracked, or broken, the society that rests upon it will be in grave danger. The saga of a nation is the saga of its families written large.

Whoever owns the family owns the future.

When the family structure breaks down, all manner of calamity and chaos enter into society. When the family breaks down, crime goes up, poverty goes up, abuse goes up. When the family breaks down, gender confusion and role confusion go up. I could go on, but you get the point.

It is the role of civil government to promote and protect the family as God created it to be. This role is critical because the family serves as the foundation for the stability of the nation. Statistics demonstrate holistically that when families are intact—no matter the nation—crime is down, productivity is up, and peace is prevalent.

When wrong or false definitions undermine the roles in the family and the purpose of the family according to God's prescribed way, we witness the devolution of society. This is especially apparent whenever the government takes an active role in seeking to undermine and replace the structure of the family itself.

In Isaiah 3:12 and 25–26, God gives us a glimpse of what happens when He is removed from society and His prescribed order for the family is removed from a nation. We read:

O My people! Their oppressors are children,
And women rule over them.
O My people! Those who guide you lead you astray
And confuse the direction of your paths. (v. 12)

Your men will fall by the sword
And your mighty ones in battle.
And her gates will lament and mourn,
And deserted she will sit on the ground. (vv. 25–26)

God tells us in this passage that when the structure of the family got confused, the children became rebellious, and the women abandoned their biblical role in life and the home. Men became passive and weak to such a degree that the structures of society collapsed and fell. Even if we go all the way back to Genesis 6, we are given a view of the evil breakdown of the family. When men became demonized and married women who then gave birth to demonically influenced children, violence broke out in all the earth. The inhabitants of the land became so wicked and immoral that God even regretted having made them. He says in Genesis 6:7, "I will blot out man whom I have created from the face of the land, from man to animals to creeping things and to birds of the sky; for I am sorry that I have made them."

God literally destroyed all of humanity, barring one family, with the flood because the foundation of the family and thus the foundation of society had become ruined. Society devolved to the point of destruction.

In order to reboot society, God returned to His original plan. He started it all over again. And He did so with a family. God had informed Noah that He would send a flood but that He would also establish His covenant through him. In this way, God had Noah enter the ark with his sons and his wife and his sons' wives, along with every living creature represented in groups of two. The two were to reflect a male and a female because without this gender representation, the creature would become extinct.

The breakdown of the family is not an inconsequential situation. The distortion of gender roles is not a mere sideshow. Our entire future as a nation is banking on the family unit remaining intact and being able to survive the onslaught of the enemy's tactics. But when the government joins hands with the enemy in order to seek to work against the family as well—through undermining it, redefining it, or trying to replace it—we as believers in Jesus Christ must take a stand politically. We cannot expect healing in our land if we turn a blind eye to the targeted attack on God's definition of the family.

The family structure is to set the pace for which society was created. Government does not own the family. Government has no children. God owns the family, and He owns it by creative fiat. In other words, He decided that it would exist and so He determined what it would be. He only backs what He created and when His creation abides by how He created us to function. If we choose to go our own way, we pick up the tab to fix the issues that arise.

When you purchase a product from the store, they often give you a manufacturer's warranty. What this warranty states, without saying so directly, is that they stand behind the product. They back what they created. They warrant the viability of their product because they are willing to assume the costs should it break.

However, a warranty can become void. This happens when the user of the product decides to do something different with it than was originally intended. If a person takes a toaster, for example, and uses it as a baking pan in the oven rather to heat up toast on its own, then the toaster will no longer be under warranty. This is because a warranty remains valid only if the item is used according to its created purposes.

Similarly, God has warrantied society to work by virtue of the family structure. When the government, or any entity or individual for that matter, decides that the family should be about something other than what God has determined, society loses out on the warranty. When society loses the warranty, society is no longer covered. God is only going to stand by the product He created based on the reason why He created it. There will be no spiritual bailouts for a society gone astray from God's intended purposes.

GOD'S INTENDED PURPOSES

To understand God's intended purposes for the family, we need to look at Genesis 1. In this chapter, we read that God decided to make mankind in His own image. In verses 26–27 we read,

> Then God said, "Let Us make man in Our image, according to Our likeness; and let them rule over the fish of the sea and over the birds of the sky and over the cattle and over all the earth, and over every creeping thing that creeps on the earth." God created man in His own image, in the image of God He created him; male and female He created them.

In this opening chapter to all of Scripture, God lays out the principle for the family structure. There would be a male, and there would be a female. When the two joined together to form a family, God intended for them to be fruitful and multiply. He wants the family unit to then expand His likeness throughout the earth. He also says in this passage that He has created the family to rule. Thus, we find in this one passage the three reasons for the family.

First, the family is a reflection of God because we are made in His image. The family is to mirror God. That means the family is to reflect the distinct merging of unity while retaining of personality that shows up in the Trinity of God the Father, the Son, and the Holy Spirit. To better understand the Trinity, I like to compare it to a pretzel where there are three holes. The first hole is not the second hole nor is the second hole the third hole, but they are all tied together by the same dough.

When God explained how He would enter history, the Father sent the Son. Then, when the Son left the time line of history, He sent the Spirit. There existed this progression of the unit of the theistic family in heaven manifesting itself on earth. That's why we should not be surprised when we see God's plan for the family. God created Adam, and then He took a rib from Adam in order to create Eve. Lastly, out of Eve came the children who would then go on to reproduce in the same way. Each family unit is to reflect the unity yet distinctiveness of the triune God.

In fact, so deep is this concept in the psyche of humanity that even our government has tried to reflect the triune God with the three areas of government. We have the Judicial branch, the Legislative branch, and the Executive branch. The main difference, though, is that the biblical Trinity always acts in unity. There is no conflict. Thus, when the family was established, it was established to reflect the unifying cooperation of the Godhead. The family wasn't created just so people could be happy. Blessing from God would come about based on people fulfilling why God created the family. The family was first and foremost to be a reflection of God Himself.

Second, the family was created so that we could replicate God's reflection throughout the earth. When God instructed the family to be fruitful and multiply, He was establishing a generational plan whereby He would spread His image worldwide. God chose to fill the earth with His reflection through the multiplying effect of the family. Children do not exist just so parents can have look-alikes. Children have been given to us so that God's image can have look-alikes. God replicates His character, purposes, and plans throughout the world as families reproduce and raise children in His likeness and according to His kingdom worldview.

Third, the family was given to the world to exercise God's rule on earth. Families are to raise children to understand and love the law of God—the primary law under Jesus Christ, being that of loving God and loving others—so that the character of God serves as the over-arching rule on earth (Luke 10:27; Matt. 22:35–40; Deut. 6:1–18). Thus, families reflect, replicate, and rule as a result of God's vested care and provision to them.

The government exists to protect the family. It should protect the replication of children as well as recognize the sovereignty of families in ruling according to God's righteous and just laws within their divinely ordained realms of jurisdiction and influence. Yet we have seen anything but this protection in our nation, and in many nations, throughout the world. Which is why we live in a world dominated by chaos, conflict, war, poverty, and despair.

Keep in mind, it's important to note that God began to set a process for the establishment of families with a single person. He didn't start with a marriage. He began it all by creating a single male, Adam. The reason for this is because He wanted the single person to be complete in Him until they became a married person. Single doesn't just mean unmarried in God's economy. Single means complete until marriage. If you get two incomplete singles coming together, you just create an incomplete marriage. God never meant for a single person who is unmarried to be incomplete.

A person is complete under God when he or she fulfills their divinely designed purpose for being. The problem is that when sin entered the world, death entered with it because death is the consequence of sin's impact on society. What evil did as it permeated the lives of individuals—singles and married couples—was take what God had established and contorted it. Evil distorted the grand design of God's plan for humanity. Evil opened the door for governmental interference as well as individual license. People cohabit in today's world, rather than choose to commit to marriage, like they are visiting a car dealership wanting to take a test drive before they purchase the vehicle. Yet God ordained marriage to serve as a reflection of His unity within the Trinity itself.

In God's ordained plan for marriage, a couple married in order to date. A couple entered marriage in order to fulfill a lifetime commitment under God. God prescribed what role the husband was supposed to be in the home. God laid out what the woman was supposed to do in the home. By working together, a husband and wife were to establish an environment in which children could be raised to follow God and reflect His image in society.

Government was never designed as an entity to interfere with the home. The role of the government is to protect the family unit from outside destructive forces. It should support God's definition of the family. The Bible declares in Malachi 2:14–16 that a husband and wife are married based on a covenantal agreement. We read,

> "Yet you say, 'For what reason?' Because the LORD has been a witness between you and the wife of your youth, against whom you have dealt treacherously, though she is your companion and your wife by covenant. But not one has done so who has a remnant of the Spirit. And what did that one do while he was seeking a godly offspring? Take heed then to your spirit, and let no one deal treacherously against the wife

of your youth. For I hate divorce," says the LORD, the God of Israel, "and him who covers his garment with wrong," says the LORD of hosts. "So take heed to your spirit, that you do not deal treacherously."

Marriage is a covenantal agreement. A covenant is a divinely created relational bond. Covenants are significant in God's kingdom order. In fact, God's kingdom is run by His covenant. There are four areas of covenantal rule, which include the individual, family, church, and civil government. When God established His various covenants, He was setting up the rules by which each was to function. In order to advance His rule in society, the entities within each covenantal sphere need to align themselves with His prescribed ways.

Whenever someone, or something, messes with the covenant, they've endangered God's flow of blessing into the world. The reason why is because covenants are relational bonds. In order for God to provide His blessing through the covenant, the other entities in the covenant need to be in alignment with Him. The problem is that men have decided what they want manhood to be. Women have decided what they want womanhood to be. Society has decided what they want the definition of the family to be. As a result, we have absolute chaos in our world today. Chaos in the family shows up as chaos in the society. And unfortunately, Christians have joined in on the redefining of all these covenantal rules and relationships, thus making the church lose her ability to influence the culture for Christ at the level she was intended to.

CHALLENGES TO GOD'S PURPOSE

Whenever the government or politicians conflict with God's prescribed order, the government will lose. Society will lose. God will unleash His reaction to our rebellion, the result of which will be unbearable for many. This is why Christians must support politicians and policies that promote and protect the family as God designed it to be.

One example would be the government's instituting of no-fault divorce. Jesus made it clear in Scripture that there is no such thing as a no-fault divorce. Yet when the government decides to step in and redefine what the family should look like, the ripple effects become tsunamic in nature. Far too many people go to the church for a marriage but to civil government for the divorce. God doesn't condone divorce simply because two people are overstressed or unhappy. He urges married couples to focus on what they need to do in order to strengthen their families and reflect His image as they should. Divorce should be very difficult to obtain, not cheap or easy. In addition, marriages should be heterosexual and not homosexual.

Instead of pursuing God's purpose for the family, we have parents shuffling children from house to house. Or children being raised in foster care where the government now must become the parent. We have children who are being abandoned or abused, leaving them to grow up confused only to later contribute to the chaos of society. We have a culture that has lost its conscience to such a degree that right and wrong appear as topics to debate. One of the reasons we must voice our values in the public square when it comes to politics and how governments should protect the family unity is because without it, we have a generation of people who no longer understand standards of absolute truth.

This has been further introduced through government-led education for our children. We witness schools now teaching things that undermine our Creator. The government has stepped in to act where the parents should in the raising of their kids. In many ways we see public education overruling parents' desires for their kids. Oftentimes, they give out information that rebels against God, such as the teaching of evolution no longer even as a theory but as fact. Rather than presenting multiple theories like evolution and creationism side by side so that children can have a knowledge base by which to discern truth, public education has become much more like a political arm for propaganda.

We've also seen the introduction of sex education into younger and younger grades, whether that comes through the handing out of condoms, or teaching that families can be comprised of two daddies or two mommies, the educational system funded by our government is now in outright opposition to God and His rules. In fact, simply saying "God bless America" and playing the song at school events has become an issue in many locations.

There are systems being set up that are government-run that seek to undermine the family as well as redefine the values that come from a theistic worldview. By taking politics and policies seriously, kingdom followers of Jesus Christ discover the need to stand up for options such as school choice or homeschooling. Parents should have a lead voice in the education for their children. They are to make sure that what children are being taught is consistent with the truth (Deut. 4:9–10; 6:4–9). Truth is God's view on every subject. When the government fails to provide an adequate voice to parents, it stands in opposition to God. Whenever an entity opposes God, it has declared itself to be a pagan institution. Our nation has become paganized. What's worse, when kingdom-minded voters fail to prioritize the research and strategic nature of their votes, we have embraced and encouraged the paganization of our land. When God is removed from education, truth is in trouble and lies become its replacement. This is why school choice should be advocated by kingdom parents.

Until we prioritize the family in our public policies, we will continue to live in a culture of chaos. Malachi 4:4–6 emphasizes this

> **Until we prioritize the family in our public policies, we will continue to live in a culture of chaos.**

reality by showing us that God cursed the land due to the family structure being in disarray. It's not too far off to state that our land is cursed in many ways today due to the failure of families to raise children according to kingdom values.

Until we get back to God's definition of the family, and the civil government supporting that definition, we will suffer as a society.

Satan successfully reversed the roles in the family in Genesis 3. He got the man to be a passive participant in the home. Eve became the aggressive dictator. Adam failed but tried to blame his failure on Eve. That's when God reinforced His prescribed roles because He held Adam responsible. As a result of this rebellion within the family, the children wound up violent. Cain killed Abel, which introduced the first incident of human bloodshed on our planet. By the time you get to Genesis 6, the whole world has to be destroyed due to the immorality and evil throughout. Satan started all of that simply by undermining God's Word and flipping the roles in the family.

Until we get back to God's definition of the family, and the civil government supporting that definition, we will suffer as a society. In fact, in Mark 6:14–29, we read about John the Baptist condemning a political ruler for an unlawful marriage. John the Baptist used his voice to speak against the atrocities of the governing authorities and how those atrocities were spilling out into society. Just like John the Baptist confronted the political rulers of his day, we must also be willing to confront the governing authorities and political leaders concerning things on which God has spoken clearly. When it comes to matters of marriage and family and how both are to function, God has not stuttered.

God has made it clear that families are to stay together. Families are to take care of their own. You are to take care of your mother or your father as they age. You are to help your kids as they transition into parenthood themselves. You are to fight for your marriage, fight for your family (Neh. 4:14), and do what you need to do in order to strengthen your home as well as the homes within your extended family unit. What's more, we as believers and followers of Jesus Christ need to call to account the politicians and governing officials so that they will enact and enforce policies to strengthen and promote the family bond.

We must proactively support the development of families, especially the responsibility of men to care for their families. That's one reason why God would call the men to spend time with Him three times a year so that He could lift them up as they are to lead others (Ex. 34:23–24). After calling the men to Himself, God would send them back home so that the nation itself would prosper and be saved. What our government needs to do, and our politicians need to promote, is valuing women, yes, but also of holding our men to account. If a baby-daddy doesn't need to be in the home to help the home because government assistance and welfare makes it more profitable for him to be away, then we need to elect politicians who will seek to change such policies. Men must be held responsible for the families they are helping to create.

In fact, in Scripture it was the men who were responsible for raising the children (Eph. 6:4). The women were present alongside to help, but never to replace. God told Abraham in Genesis 18:19 that He had chosen him to become a great nation. He was to see to the raising of the next generation of his own legacy through instilling a standard of righteousness and justice. Fathers are to transfer a moral standing with God (righteousness) as well as an equitable standard among people (justice). Families are needed to raise children without prejudice. Fathers are needed to raise boys who will grow up and treat women the right way. Mothers are needed to instill godly character qualities in the future women of our nation. And policies are needed to support families to do these things.

I'll never forget the role my father played in my life. Despite having to work multiple jobs just to keep a roof over our heads and food on our plates, my father never quit. Even when my mother would give him a hard time, he held on to his faith in God. He held on to his love for his family. He kept praying for my mother until she became saved herself. He kept loving her despite her nagging. He was kind to her despite her failure to reciprocate the kindness. He did all of this in faith that God would bring about a change in her heart, according to His Word. And He did just that.

My life, as well as the lives of my children, grandchildren, and great-grandchildren, have gone an entirely new direction due to my father's unwavering commitment to God and family. We need more men like my father who will press through when the going gets tough. But what we also need are more believers standing up to voice the value of policies that protect the family. We need policies that preserve marriage, rather than those that seek to divide it. We need government-assistance related to staying together or producing positive outcomes in the home, rather than just in producing unwanted, neglected babies. We don't want kids to be wards of the state. The state was not created by God to raise our families.

We must, however, not neglect the many single-parent families who are doing the best they can to fill in the gaps in order to have a stable home. In their case, the civil government should provide a safety net that seeks to address needs in the cases where there is no extended family or private-sector support to the meeting of those needs that they cannot address themselves.

THE GOVERNMENT'S RESPONSIBILITY TO FAMILIES

We must return to a national governance whereby the politicians and policies seek to promote and protect the family as God defined it. Once we leave God's definition of the family, we can kiss the culture goodbye. We can say goodbye to our nation. We can say goodbye to safety and prosperity and peace.

Joshua made it clear in Joshua 24:15 that he and his family would serve the Lord. It starts with one home. It starts with one man. One mother. One politician. One voter. One person choosing to use his or her platform of influence to impact culture on behalf of the preservation of families. We cannot turn our children over to the culture. We will not only lose them, but we will lose what little remains of our culture as well. We cannot allow the government to define our values. God defines our values, and He determines how things are to operate and function.

If we do not get this fixed, and fixed soon, I do not want to imagine the kind of world our great-grandchildren and great-great-grandchildren will live in. When you have a government that doesn't protect and promote God's definition of the family, then you are looking at a world going to hell in a handbasket.

I heard a story once about a hunter who took his pigs to market. He had a whole herd of pigs to sell. One person asked him as he passed by how he had managed to capture so many wild pigs. He told the person inquiring that it wasn't that hard. He explained that at first he simply put out some food and the nearby pigs would come to eat. Then, after a while, he built a fence on one side of the food. The pigs ignored the fence and still came to eat. After a few days, he built another side of the fence. And then another, and then the final gate. Before they knew it, the pigs were trapped.

The pigs had come for free food while the hunter inconspicuously put up a fence to trap them in. The point being, we should be careful never to allow a governmental system to offer us so many things for free that it draws our children into a trap. Once they, or even we, get caught in a system that undermines God's righteous rule in society, we will all be taken to market.

We must do better for the futures of those who come after us. We must provide the roadmap for policies that will reinforce the power of the family in culture. We must fight for our families, and that includes fighting for them as we vote, protest, write letters to politicians, or use whatever sphere of influence God has given us to impact our culture for Christ.

Chapter 7

THE IMPORTANCE OF CHURCH

A *trick bag* is a catch-22. It's when you are caught in a situation where it seems like a lose-lose proposition. Whichever way you go, you can't win. Your back is up against the wall, and you feel stuck.

When it comes to politics and voting, a lot of people feel like they are in a trick-bag situation. If I go over here and participate with this set of policies and politicians, I'm going to lose some ideals and compromise some beliefs. Or if I go over here and participate with this other set of policies and politicians, I'll also lose some ideals and compromise some beliefs. There has never been a time in our nation where politics has been more polarizing. It almost seems like a trap that breeds division. It certainly stirs up conflict anywhere and everywhere. People argue about policies and politicians now more than I've ever seen in my seven decades on earth.

That's why it is more important than ever to find out what God says on the matter of politics. Once you do, you may discover that choosing sides isn't the best option. You may wind up like many who are now declaring themselves to be independents. Or, even better, there are those who now understand that they are to be kingdom independents—those who want to honor God in this area of politics.

If you recall in August of 2005, a devastating hurricane hit our land. They called her Katrina. New Orleans was laid to waste due to this serious and damaging storm. But Katrina did not cause all the destruction on her own. No, it was made worse by one thing—the levees failing. The levees had been set up to hold back the water from entering the city, but on this particular day they did not do their job. As a result, society in New Orleans was shattered. This took place not only because the storm raged but also because the systems set up to hold back its wrath failed.

When you and I, or collectively all of us as a nation, fail to give God His due in our culture, our national levees will fail. Storms, which we could have weathered, will prove devastating to us because we have circumvented that which was established to provide us with protection.

God has a levee in our land. He has a mechanism to inform society through the government on how it is supposed to work. If that levy fails and government rules on its own apart from His guidance and will, we can expect to see the shattering of our society. The levee God has placed within our society is His church. When religious freedom is denied, the church is muzzled, or it fails to function in its divinely authorized role—then tyranny reigns.

This is not to say that the church is the government, or the church should govern the government, but the church should be the model and conscience for how a society is to function. Without the church being the church Christ died to establish, chaos and calamity will rule in the culture.

GOD AND GOVERNMENT

Before we get much deeper into this chapter, I want you to know that I know that this subject makes many people uncomfortable. When they hear someone discussing the church and its relationship to the civil government in a land, the red flags of church and state pop up everywhere. Yet while the legitimate establishment of the "separation of church and state" holds value, it is never to be confused with the separation of God and government. There should be institutional separation of church and state, certainly. But there should never be the separation of God and government. This is because civil government is God's established covenantal institution for providing and protecting an orderly, righteous, and just society. He has set political leaders in place as His ministers to rule on matters of state.

In Matthew 22, we witness Jesus being put in a trick bag regarding political allegiances. The Pharisees had come to Him and plotted on how they might trap Him in His words. For those of you who may not know, the Pharisees would have been considered the religious conservatives of their day. But the Pharisees didn't come alone on this particular day. They came with the Herodians. The Herodians would have been considered the politicians. So, essentially, we find both the religious conservatives and the politicians teaming up on Jesus.

Both sides come together to try to trap Him by presenting to Him the following scenario. We read in verses 15–17:

> Then the Pharisees went and plotted together how they might trap Him in what He said. And they sent their disciples to Him, along with the Herodians, saying, "Teacher, we know that You are truthful and teach the way of God in truth, and defer to no one; for You are not partial to any. Tell us then, what do You think? Is it lawful to give a poll-tax to Caesar, or not?"

The two groups were asking Jesus to vote. They wanted to know if He would vote on a tax bill of sorts. We see both the secular and the religious ganging up on Jesus, asking Him to weigh in on a poll tax. The reason why they felt it was a good trap was because if Jesus said that everyone was to pay the poll tax than He would be affirming the oppressor, since Rome was oppressing the Jews. He would be backing the continuation of oppression due to illegitimate taxation. But if Jesus said not to pay the poll tax, then they could accuse Him of being subversive to the Roman government. Either way He chose to answer, they thought they had Him.

But Jesus surprised them. He asked them to show Him the coin that would be used to pay the poll tax. When they did, He asked, "Whose likeness is on this?" To that they responded that the likeness was that of Caesar. Caesar would be considered a similar position of authority as the president in the United States. Thus, the head (or figurehead) of government was on the coin.

That's when Jesus hit them with a zinger. He replied, "'Then render to Caesar the things that are Caesar's; and to God the things that are God's.' And hearing this, they were amazed, and leaving Him, they went away" (vv. 21–22). The Pharisees and politicians hadn't asked Him about that. They had asked Him to choose. But Jesus replied in a way they could not condemn because the government supplies goods and services in exchange for a tax. Jesus encouraged them to pay to the government what belonged to the government for those benefits. But He also instructed them to give to God what was God's.

Jesus gave them a "God and government" response. He was not about to leave God out of the taxing question or the political trap they sought to place Him in. Jesus rightfully brought God in even though those seeking to trip Him up never even asked about God at all. The reason Jesus introduced God into the equation was because He understood, as every Christian should understand, that it is a believer's role to represent God's perspective and His rule in government. We are not to apologize for aligning with the God who created and instituted government in the first place. We are to pay our taxes, yes. After all, it is the government's currency with the leaders' images on it. We get benefits from the government such as roads, civil services, education, and protection. But we are never to stop there. That's part of the discussion, but not its entirety. The image on the coin may be the likeness of a man, but the image of a man is the likeness of God (Gen. 1:26–27).

We are often persuaded not to bring religion into political debates or policies. But Jesus answered clearly to this challenge when He said that we should. God is part of the equation. One way we illustrate this is through the placement of the inaugurated president's hand on the Bible. God is both the initiator and the concluder. But what we also must keep in mind is that He is to be a part of everything else in between.

God is the only lawgiver, and He is the ultimate judge.

People often don't mind if God is involved in the invocation and the benediction. They just don't want Him as part of the discussion about laws, righteousness, or justice. But Scripture tells us clearly that He must be a part of those discussions. After all, "There is only one Lawgiver and Judge, the One who is able to save and to destroy; but who are you who judge your neighbor?" (James 4:12).

God is the only lawgiver, and He is the ultimate judge. That's why anytime we have a discussion on civil government, we must bring God and His perspective to the table to determine what should be legal or illegal, just or unjust, righteous or unrighteous. It is an insult for a Christian to leave God's person and policies out of the equation or conversations on politics. What's more, it is an insult for the church, and its leaders, to do the same.

We are to honor Caesar, but we are not to leave God out. Caesar is responsible for government. But God is responsible for everything. We are reminded of this throughout the Bible:

The LORD has established His throne in the heavens,
And His sovereignty rules over all. (Ps. 103:19)

For the kingdom is the LORD's
And He rules over the nations. (Ps. 22:28)

The Most High is ruler over the realm of mankind and be-
stows it on whomever He wishes. (Dan. 4:25b)

God's perspective should never be left out of the political discussion, even when His name is not brought up by those around
you. You bring it up. Jesus brought it up because government needs
divine influence if it is going to govern rightly for the benefit of its
citizens. It doesn't just need God's name or the symbolism of the
Bible, it needs God's policies and His guidelines. Government must
be informed about what Scripture has to say on matters of social
engagement, protection, and provision.

THE CHURCH AND POLITICS

Christians need to stop apologizing or punking out when it comes to
politics. We are not called to apologize. We are called to testify. We
are called to influence legislators and legislation. Whenever God and
His ways are removed from politics, 1 Samuel 8:10–18 tells us that
government will continue to grow until it becomes the new false god.
Government was never meant to be god. There is only one God, and
it is not the government. When the government conflicts with God,
society will suffer the results.

That's why there must be freedom of religion to provide the opportunity to allow spiritual influence in the society. Anything that
infringes upon the freedom of a person's religion must be rejected.
It must be stopped. Anything that prevents believers or the church

from representing God and His will in the culture must be opposed. If it is not, the hurricane of racism, elitism, classism, or any other issue will flood and do damage because the levee of God's rule is no longer allowed to do what it was intended to do.

According to the Bible, civil government is supposed to be limited and not allowed to overrule God

We are not to align politically, we are to align spiritually.

(Mark 12:13–17). The authority vested in the government has been given to them by God. Government has been set up as an institution that submits to God's overarching rules. When they choose not to function according to the original intention, they and their country suffer as a result. The church has been placed in history to be an influence in the governing affairs of man. We are not to align politically, we are to align spiritually. It is the church's role to speak into politics by providing God's viewpoint on a matter. God has spoken on every category that pertains to life, family, community, and government. Yet because the church has decided to be more cultural than Christian, we have become followers and not influencers where we are needed most.

In Ezekiel 43, God issued a complaint about how things were being run at that time. He let them know that they had stepped out of bounds when there was an illegitimate relationship of church and state. We read about this where it states,

> Then I heard one speaking to me from the house, while a man was standing beside me. He said to me, "Son of man, this is the place of My throne and the place of the soles of My feet, where I will dwell among the sons of Israel forever. And the house of Israel will not again defile My holy name, neither they nor their kings, by their harlotry and by the corpses of

their kings when they die, by setting their threshold by My threshold and their door post beside My door post, with only the wall between Me and them. And they have defiled My holy name by their abominations which they have committed. So I have consumed them in My anger. Now let them put away their harlotry and the corpses of their kings far from Me; and I will dwell among them forever." (vv. 6–9)

This is one of the clearest passages in Scripture where God makes His view known on government. He tells them they have brought their governing kings too close to Him. He lets the people know in no uncertain terms that they have brought their political ideas, personalities, and ideologies too close to His own. There exist no multiple sets of kings in God's kingdom. There is only one King and one Lawgiver. We are not to bring the culture's viewpoints into the church in order to influence the body of Christ. No, we are to bring God's viewpoint from God's temple, the church, into the culture. Somehow, we have gotten these two things turned around.

It is God who usurps presidents. It is God who usurps Congress. His rule is the rule of the land, and it is to stand. When presidents, Congress, or other politicians go against His rule, they and the people will suffer consequences. Politicians are never to be considered equal to God. They may think they control the agenda, but they do not control the outcome. It is the role of the church to be the conscience of the culture. God chided the inhabitants in this passage in Ezekiel because they chose to bring politics' influence into the temple. The temple is God's dwelling place. It was the center of Israel's life. All of life revolved around it—not just the so-called spiritual components of life.

The temple led the way in the areas of social experiences, politics, family, and even the economy. The temple influenced it all. But when the people began to drag the political agendas into God's temple as if they could compete with God for allegiance, God let them know they had gone too far. Today, the church is God's temple (Eph. 2:21–22) that should affect every area of life (Eph. 1:22–23).

THE CHURCH'S INFLUENCE

The church has become too political in the way it adopts and absorbs the agendas of the culture and political parties. The church is now anemic when it comes to making an impact for God and for good. The church is supposed to be like an embassy representing in a foreign land the rule of the authority to which it belongs. The church is supposed to be a little bit of heaven a long way from home. We are to reflect God's viewpoint—not the Democrats' viewpoint. We are to reflect God's priorities—not the Republicans' priorities. We are to align ourselves under God, not acquiesce to political parties. It is idolatry to do otherwise.

God reminds us in Ezekial 43 that if we desire His presence and power to be among us, we better have a clear line of demarcation between the culture's politics and politicians and His divine authority. That doesn't mean we aren't to talk about politics in a church setting, or that we shouldn't have political forums. It does mean, however, that we are to inform politics and cultural issues from the Word of God, not the other way around. We have got this whole thing backward these days. That's why it is important to support people and policies that undergird the freedom of the church to *be* the church. Anything that infringes upon it through illegitimate restrictions or dumbing down the kingdom purpose of the church by turning it into a three-ring circus for entertainment purposes only must be opposed. There are so many churches today where you can't really tell if you have gone to church or to a concert with a motivational speaker added on top. Culture has so invaded God's temple that it has become difficult to locate God in many churches.

Yet when the church is strengthened to the point of discipling her members to comprehensively align with God's Word, our culture can influence the world for good. The church, however, is not only to disciple its members but the Great Commission commands it to disciple the nations (Matt. 28:16–20). This means that God's people should be affecting the atmosphere and structures of society that govern how people live. Many churches and Christians have too narrow of a view of kingdom discipleship. Secular nations should benefit from the presence of God's people in their midst (Jer. 29:4–7).

If you look at the civil rights movement as an example, the church rose up and stood together to speak righteousness and justice into the society. God blessed this movement to enact great legal changes because it was done according to His principles and priorities. When we rise up on our own accord as fractured and fissured groups here or there and do so out of alignment with God's prescribed principles, we may make a loud noise, but we will have no lasting results for good. In fact, we may even find ourselves worse off than before.

Only when the kingdom of God takes precedence in how a society is to run will we be able to live as a free, righteous, just, and productive nation. God has spoken on every subject, and He has not stuttered. Yet because far too many of us hold such a low view of God, the levees of His sovereign care have shattered. Second Chronicles 15:3–6 reminds us that when we leave God out of our culture, we will have conflict. We will not find peace. We will experience chaos on all fronts. Collective Christianity is to promote God's systems, rules, and laws. When we fail to do that, and do it well, we yield to Satan's whims and God's wrath.

The church is critical to a nation's success. That's why Paul tells Timothy as a pastor to instruct his church to pray for government leaders and all men. We read this in 1 Timothy 2,

> First of all, then, I urge that entreaties and prayers, petitions and thanksgivings, be made on behalf of all men, for kings and all who are in authority, so that we may lead a tranquil and quiet life in all godliness and dignity. This is good and

acceptable in the sight of God our Savior, who desires all men to be saved and to come to the knowledge of the truth. (vv. 1–4)

Timothy was to preach the principles and precepts of God, especially with regard to how the church should function in society. To abandon the Word of God because of political expedience by any party is to shoot yourself in the foot. The church and her members should never abandon their biblically informed conscience for political gain. The church doesn't exist for politics. It exists for the kingdom of God.

Matthew 16:18–19 reminds us of the significance of the church,

> "I also say to you that you are Peter, and upon this rock I will build My church; and the gates of Hades will not overpower it. I will give you the keys of the kingdom of heaven; and whatever you bind on earth shall have been bound in heaven, and whatever you loose on earth shall have been loosed in heaven."

The church exists as an extension of heavenly authority on earth and is designed to bring God's legislative influence and biblical solutions from heaven into history, since it alone has been given the keys of special authoritative access into His presence (Isa. 22:22). But somewhere along the way we seemed to have lost our way. How can we have all these churches on all these corners with all these programs and all these ministries led by all these ministers in all these buildings promoting all this activity, yet still have all this mess? There's a dead monkey on the line somewhere. The reason I say that is because we have this mess due to the church no longer being the church. We are merely a religious gathering—a social club. What good is a sports team with brand-new uniforms, a brand-new stadium, and brand-new equipment if they only keep losing? They may have spent a lot of money, but they are still losers at the end of the day.

Similarly, what good is a church with brand-new buildings, brand-new food trucks, and brand-new music and visual arts systems, but they still keep losing in the culture? If there is no impact, influence, or insertion of kingdom values into the land, they are nothing more than a highly priced losing entity. If we don't see communities being upgraded, economic and racial justice being obtained, relationships being mended, families being saved, then what is the point in paying for all the buildings and salaries just to keep a social club going?

Something is truly wrong in the church today. In so many ways we have devolved into a social agency with a little Jesus sprinkled on top. We're spending too much of our time, thoughts, and conversations on what the politicians are doing that we have lost the opportunity to share what God would want done. It is only when we kick out the imposters like God indicated in Ezekiel 47 that we will open the floodgates of God's power, provision, and blessing once again. He says that when we remove the cultural rulers from influencing God's temple, then the water of God's presence and power will flow.

Water is a life-giving substance. When it flowed into the temple in this passage, it then went down into the street and community. It brought life to anything and everything it touched. That is how God has designed His blessing and favor to flow. It starts at the church when a church is in alignment with God, and then it flows into the community and the nation. God does not skip the church house to fix the White House. Rather, God desires to use the church to influence the powers that be (Eph. 3:10).

God designed things so that the life-giving essence would flow from Him to the church and then through the church onto the streets and into the community. His love and presence would address and heal the racial tensions, social divide, political schisms, and everything else. The greatest example of this in the history of our nation is the black church during slavery. There were no government grants, no federal programs, no cultural support, and yet the church not only hewed out a religious order, it also created schools, social service agencies, newspapers, colleges, banks, and more. All of that came from the church because the church was looking to God for direction.

If God was able to do that through the black church that had only a minimal amount of governmental support, what do you think God can do today if the church were to truly act as the salt and light He has called us to be (Matt. 5:13–16)? We should be leveraging influence in our culture in order to bring about good for others and the advancement of God's kingdom agenda on earth. The church exists to promote the kingdom by bringing biblical solutions to our secular society. This is why civil government must protect religious freedom and why the church should pray and righteously insist that it does so (1 Tim. 2:2).

When I was the chaplain for the Dallas Cowboys under Coach Tom Landry, I would work out with the team before their official workout began. I would catch passes from Roger Staubach and Danny White, as well as run routes with the players before we would head in for chapel. Because I was out there on the field participating so much, I got to know some of the plays. One of the plays was a simple fly pattern. For you non-football readers, a *fly pattern* is where the wide receiver speeds ahead to run straight down the field in order for the quarterback to throw a long pass. The goal is for him to catch the pass and score a touchdown in one play. In other words, the fly pattern wasn't about trying to just get another first down. They were trying to go for the big score in just one play.

That's why the receivers had to be so fast. If a receiver could outrun the guy covering him, he would be able to give space for the quarterback to the throw the ball in a location that wouldn't be defended or picked off. The problem with the play, though, is that it takes just a bit longer than the other plays to unwind. This is because the quarterback has to give time to the receiver to get downfield.

Sometimes the other team would blitz the play. Also for you non-football readers, a *blitz* is where the linebackers from the other team, or the defensive back, would try to tackle the quarterback before he had a chance to throw. That was one way to stop the fly pattern from being successful.

In addition to the fly pattern, I also learned about the waggle. Now, a *waggle* was where the running back would peel off to the side just in case the quarterback got in trouble and was not able to throw the long ball for the fly pattern. If the other team was blitzing or the receiver was too well-covered, there needed to be another option. This is when the quarterback would turn to the side and toss the ball to the halfback. The halfback had waggled (moved) to the other side as a safety plan. When the quarterback threw the ball to the halfback, the halfback would still try to score a touchdown, but his route had become an option since the original play could not work out.

God called a fly pattern for Israel when He installed them as His kingdom agency. He said He wanted to score on the long ball to Israel. They were to catch the ball and bring in the kingdom of Jesus Christ and His rule on earth. This play would be a long play to develop. It would span many years leading to the birth of the Savior and His life on earth. The problem was that Satan blitzed the play. Satan got into the backfield to stop the program of God. They got to Jesus Christ and crucified Him on Good Friday. Satan and his cohorts wanted to end the kingdom play.

But what they didn't realize was that there was a waggle. God had created another option. The option was the church. He said that even though Israel had rejected Him, He was going to designate another receiver. He would build His church and they would waggle (move) off to the side.

Thus, even though Israel couldn't receive the ball because of Satan's blitz, God had another group He chose to toss the ball to in order to advance down the field. It was the church of the living God and He wanted them to reach up and grab the kingdom in order to still score a touchdown for the rule of God in history. This means that the church should never become politized if it expects to experience God's authority in history.

You and I have been given the kingdom ball and it is up to us not to drop it. We are to protect this ball and not fumble it. We shouldn't give the ball to the other team. It's time for the church to stop handing kingdom balls to Democrats. We are to stop handing kingdom balls to Republicans. We are to stop handing kingdom balls to culture. We are kingdom citizens called by God Himself to march down the field of play called earth, our nation, or even politics, in order to score for God. We do not represent or play for the kingdoms of this world. We represent and play for the kingdom of the Lord Jesus Christ. We need to start acting like it, talking like it, walking like it, serving like it, voting like it, and praying like it. We are the church of the living God and through us, the nation will feel God's power and His presence.

Chapter 8

THE SYSTEM OF ECONOMICS

You may have heard the story of the man who stole some money but was captured by the authorities. He didn't have the money with him, so they asked him where he hid it. But it turned out the man spoke another language, so they had to send for an interpreter. When the interpreter came, the authorities said, "Ask him where he hid the money."

So the interpreter asked the thief the question in his own language, and the thief replied.

"What did he say?" the authorities wanted to know.

"He said he's not telling."

The authorities became impatient and then insisted that he tell. One said, "Tell him we want to know where the money is, and we want to know now."

The interpreter repeated the question to the thief and got the same answer. "He says he isn't going to tell you."

The head of the authorities thought he would try to scare the thief into telling, so he said to the interpreter, "Tell him that if he doesn't tell us where the money is then we are going to shoot him."

The interpreter repeated the threat to the thief, who got scared and told the interpreter step-by-step exactly where he could find the money. The authorities listened to the conversation and then asked the interpreter, "Well, what did he say?"

"He said he isn't going to tell you anything," the interpreter answered.

When it comes to the issue of money (just like in that story), I'm afraid our interpretations—and our motives—sometimes get mixed up. But money is part of God's kingdom agenda for us, and you knew we would not be able to talk about the business of government, politics, and the kingdom without dealing with the economics of the kingdom.

In fact, I hope you are getting the message by now that nothing sits outside the scope of God's kingdom. Economic issues are just as much a part of our kingdom work as anything else we could name. There should be no dichotomy between God and money. "In God We Trust" is more than a slogan on our currency. Mankind was created with the divine mandate to cultivate and protect God's creation for the benefit of humanity. This was to be done under divine guidance that involved maximum freedom, limited regulations, and strict consequences for disobedience. Thus, civil government's economic policy should be a free market driven with limited regulations, coupled with incentive productivity in a safe and responsible way, along with strict consequences for economic lawbreaking (Gen. 2:15–18).

Civil government has the divinely authorized responsibility to promote economic growth since it is to function as God's servant for good (Rom. 13:4), and that includes the fulfillment of God's original purpose of making the earth productive (Gen. 1:28). Let's see what it means for the civil government and politicians to operate economically on a kingdom agenda.

The foundation of an economic view with regard to politics grows out of God's kingdom agenda for His people and His world. This foundation reveals how God empowers His people for the righteous use of the earth's resources for profitably and (morally) conducting business as His stewards.

Let me start laying that foundation with a critical text on the subject of economics and wealth. In Deuteronomy 8, Moses addressed the Israelites on the eve of their entrance into Canaan. He recounted God's goodness to them all the way from their departure from Egypt to the present moment, which was almost forty years later, and he warned them not to forget who provided for them.

Beginning in Deuteronomy 8:11, we discover the reason for Moses's concern. He feared that once the people settled in Canaan and started living the "good life" in the suburbs of Canaanland, they would get proud. Then they would forget that they used to be slaves and that the only reason they weren't slaves now was that God had given them everything they had (vv. 11–14).

So Moses brought the message to them and laid down an absolutely foundational principle of divine economics. The Israelites needed to keep their economics in focus because,

> "Otherwise, you may say in your heart, 'My power and the strength of my hand made me this wealth.' But you shall remember the LORD your God, for it is He who is giving you power to make wealth, that He may confirm His covenant which He swore to your fathers, as it is this day." (vv. 17–18)

The principle is simply this: any discussion of economics that does not include God is not a complete or fully accurate discussion because He is the Author of all wealth on both a personal and national level. God owns it all. As the psalmist said, "The earth is the LORD's, and all it contains, the world, and those who dwell in it" (Ps. 24:1). Communism teaches that the government owns everything. Capitalism teaches that the individual owns everything. Christianity teaches that God owns everything and has freely given it into the hands of human beings to manage, or steward, on His behalf.

Scripture is clear that private property belongs to the individual, not the government (Ex. 20:15, 17; Prov. 22:28; 23:10). This philosophy rejects the socialist and communist economic philosophy that is built on the abolition of private property leading to the redistribution of wealth and government control of economic activity. This is why the Bible authorizes punishment for stealing and restitution for damaging other people's property (Ex. 21:28–36; 22:1–15; Deut. 22:1–4; 23:24–25).

God states it clearly in Psalm 50:10 and 12 that He is the owner over all and thus what He gives to humanity is what we are to use as stewards or managers: "Every beast of the forest is Mine, the cattle on a thousand hills. . . . If I were hungry, I would not tell you; for the world is Mine, and all it contains."

And Haggai 2:8 reminds us, "'The silver is Mine, and the gold is Mine,' declares the LORD of hosts." All of this means that economics is a spiritual issue. God sets the rules for poverty and wealth (1 Sam. 2:7–8). It cannot be called secular when the owner of everything is God. Like the Israelites, everything we have is rooted in the goodness of God. We cannot discuss the politics of economics on any level, from personal to national, without putting God's perspective first. Since God is the starting and ending point of all economic discussions, we need to find out what is on His kingdom agenda for the resources He has entrusted to us and our nation.

Let's start revealing that agenda with a basic question: What is God's purpose for wealth?

The answer is found at the very end of Deuteronomy 8:18, quoted above. Moses said it was God who gave the Israelites the power to gain wealth, "that He may confirm His covenant which He swore to your fathers, as it is this day."

God gives wealth that it might be used to fulfill His divine purposes, in this case His covenant with Israel. God made a covenant with Abraham, that through Abraham "all the families of the earth shall be blessed" (Gen. 12:3). He has also made a new covenant with us through Jesus Christ. God gives you the ability, capacity, giftedness, and raw materials to produce wealth in order to confirm the covenant. Which means if you don't understand the covenant then you don't understand the purpose of wealth.

Therefore, one primary confirmation of the covenant and legitimate use of wealth is when it is used to be a blessing to somebody else. Jesus Himself said, "It is more blessed to give than to receive" (Acts 20:35).

God uses wealth as a channel through which His benefits will flow to you, and through you to others. Therefore, if all you can see is your car and your house and your wardrobe . . . if you cannot point to the ways God's blessings in your life are flowing out as blessings to others, then God has no reason to give you wealth. And if God has no reason to give you wealth, then the only way you can get it is apart from Him. But if you get it apart from Him, you will pay a heavy price for going after it. God gives His economic blessings to accomplish His purposes. It is for this reason that civil government should incentivize charity.

Since God owns all the wealth of the world and has a clear purpose for it, He gets to set the rules of who will get it and how it will be used. In 1 Samuel 2:7–8, it is clear that God is the one who makes people rich or poor, in essence saying, "I set the rules. If you follow My rules, you get My results. If you follow your rules, you get your results."

God told His people Israel, in Deuteronomy 28:12, that if they would obey His rules, He would make them a lender nation instead of a debtor nation. When you use wealth God's way, it eliminates rather than accumulates debt. Our society and our nation doesn't need to face any fiscal cliff or continue to accumulate debt if we would operate according to God's rules on managing corporate greed and promoting individual productivity.

It is important to understand that God is not against wealth. If God chooses to materially bless an individual, family, church, or nation that is operating on kingdom economic principles, there should not be any feelings of false guilt for what God Himself has given. God is more concerned with how you got what you have and how you use what you have than He is with how much you have. Now if the wealth you have is gained illegitimately, then you have reason to feel guilty. But if not, then God does not heap guilt on you.

Despite God's provision of wealth and His intentions for its use, whenever God lays out the rules for what He gives, we as sinful people have a way of subverting those rules and setting up our own. Unfortunately, because of this, we end up losing more than we could ever gain.

Our first parents found that out the hard way. Adam and Eve challenged God's ownership of His provision in the garden of Eden and made up their own rules. They decided they were going to operate independently of God's economy. But they wound up with less—far less—rather than more.

Ever since then, individuals have been cursed financially because they refuse to handle God's resources God's way. Many families are in financial disarray because they are not operating on God's economic agenda. Many churches must resort to unbiblical means to accumulate money because they are not doing it God's way. And our nation is in continual economic uncertainty today due to the trillions of dollars of debt, thus risking the future stability of those who worked to contribute to our nation's resources, because we ask civil government to do more than God has established for it.

Biblical economics is a spiritual issue regarding sin and righteousness.

The economic problems we contend with as nations in our world is not due to a lack of resources on the earth. God has packed this earth with raw materials and resources beyond our wildest imagination. Mankind was designed to cultivate and develop this wealth under God's direction and blessing because Adam was given dominion over the earth. He was to rule the earth, cultivating the resources of the earth for the glory of God and the benefit of mankind. The failure to do this is because of sin, not because the earth has run out of its resources.

Biblical economics is a spiritual issue regarding sin and righteousness. But because people think our problems are merely materialistic in nature, they don't see the solutions to our problems, which come from God and His inerrant Word.

The foundation of economics is theological. Civil government should never displace the responsibility God gives to the individual, family, or church. If we would return to God on a personal, familial, ecclesiastical, and national level, we would witness the kind of proper legitimate economic development our communities need so badly. But people and politicians have established their own rules, and we are all paying a high price for this disobedience.

Sin resulted in an economic burden on the planet (Gen. 3:17–19) that will only be fully restored when Jesus returns and sets up His kingdom rule (Amos 9:13; Isa. 35:1; 51:3; 55:13). In the meantime, God wants mankind to develop and utilize the abundant resources of the earth so that they safely and responsibly benefit mankind by enhancing their lives and increasing their well-being and productivity (Deut. 29:9).

THE HINDRANCES TO KINGDOM ECONOMICS

If God is the foundation of a kingdom economic agenda, what are the hindrances that are keeping this agenda from being realized? Why can't we see kingdom-based economic development in our communities and through governmental policies? There are a number of reasons.

Greed

Greed is a lust for material things for their own sake. Greed places the material over the spiritual, resulting in the loss of the true meaning of life (Luke 12:13–21). Greed can lead to all sorts of issues economically. In fact, the primary reason that we as a nation experienced the financial downfall in 2008 was due to the greed in the housing situation. Bad federal government social policy allowed agencies to waive normal financial requirements. Greedy lenders then gave subprime loans to greedy buyers who were purchasing outside of what they could reasonably afford long-term.

Greed is a lust for material things for their own sake.

This combination of greed led to the housing meltdown as we know it. Greed involves a lust for money, and what money can buy, at the expense of yourself or someone else.

Before we move on, though, I want to clarify that greed is not to be confused with self-interest. Self-interest is not a sin. In the book of Philippians, Paul writes, "Do not merely look out for your own personal interests, but also for the interests of others" (Phil. 2:4). He doesn't say not to look out for your own self-interests at all—he just says not to forget others and their interests while you are doing so.

Is it greedy to want a better job or a nicer car? Not necessarily. It depends on the motive that drives the desire for these things. There is nothing wrong with wanting to better yourself if it is done legitimately, and if others are not forgotten in the process.

One question that always comes up here is whether Christians should play the lottery. Well, let's say the lottery jackpot one week is ten million dollars. You wonder whether you should try for it. I would ask you, is there an agenda that God has set before you that requires you to win ten million dollars?

I suspect the answer would be no. You want the ten million

because it's a lot of money, and you would be set for life. What I'm saying is that playing the lottery is not tied to any legitimate goal. Winning the money is an end in itself, and that is evil (i.e., greed).

It is equally evil for a government to prey on the greed of its citizens by attempting to derive through gaming what it could not legitimately expect its citizens to pay in fees and taxes due to incentivizing their productivity.

The Bible makes it clear that you and I are not to be involved in any plans in which our primary motivation is to try to get rich quickly (Prov. 21:5; 28:20, 22) and bypass the process of productive work as the legitimate and primary means of obtaining wealth (Prov. 10:4). Instead of praying that we win the lottery, here's what we should be asking God for:

> Keep deception and lies far from me,
> Give me neither poverty nor riches;
> Feed me with the food that is my portion,
> That I not be full and deny You and say, "Who is the LORD?"
> Or that I not be in want and steal,
> And profane the name of my God. (Prov. 30:8–9)

The writer asked for neither riches nor poverty, but for his portion. Having too much and having too little can both lead to greed. People can be greedy, but politicians and governments can be greedy too. The arbitrary increasing of the money supply or the supply of credit is the result of the inflated hearts of government officials who seek to use civil government to do what God's kingdom agenda has not authorized it to do. Such irresponsible behavior by civil government debases currency and increases cost of goods. God is very concerned about the just balance, scales, and weights (Prov. 16:11; Lev. 19:35–37).

Envy

Envy is another sinful attitude that hinders kingdom economic development. Envy goes a step further than jealousy. Jealousy says, "I am upset because you have something that I don't have." Envy says,

> # Envy is a spiritual problem because it stems from a false view of God.

"Not only am I upset about what you have, but since I don't have it, I will either make sure you don't have it or at least you will not enjoy it."

Envy sets in motion a whole string of events that try to deny people the legitimate ownership of what they have, and it creates all manner of accompanying sin. Envy is clearly a sinful passion in the Bible. Paul said that the wicked are marked by envy (Rom. 1:29), among other things, and he added that envy must not characterize the people of God (Rom. 13:13).

Envy is a spiritual problem because it stems from a false view of God. When we are envious, we are saying that God is either not sovereign or not good, because in our view He failed to give us what we think we ought to have. Therefore, we are envious and destructive if someone else has it. The root of envy is a faulty, weak view of God.

Laziness

The Bible recognizes that some people are poor because they are lazy (Prov. 10:4, 5; 12:24; 13:4, 11). It is clear that if people wish to prosper, they must be willing to work hard, and if they are unwilling to work, they should not eat (2 Thess. 3:10). Lazy people are present rather than future oriented and must begin taking responsibility for themselves and their families. When the irresponsible poor can receive government handouts that require little or no productivity on their part, then we aid and abet their economic deterioration, as well as our own. Welfare must always be tied to workfare for those who are able to do so. This also includes denying corporate welfare and government subsidies that provide unearned financial incentives or business enterprises that don't maximize productivity.

An irresponsible, over-inflated welfare system promotes laziness in many ways. That is never how God intended things to run. The state must understand that the family and the church—including the private sector—is to be the primary agency of welfare, not the government. A welfare state is illegitimate. The government should be a safety net, not the primary ongoing means of charity for able-bodied citizens. When it does so it undermines the family and the church (including the private sector), resulting in the illegitimate expansion of civil government. Thus, tyranny, deficit spending, unsustainable debt, and high taxation will also accompany it. The state should seek to incentivize the other means of charity, not replace them. The government, then, can focus on providing a robust tax-funded system of charity for the responsible poor who, because of health, tragedy, absence of local services, age, or natural calamities, need the benefit of this safety net. In this way, the government is fulfilling its call of compassion without illegitimately inverting God's covenantal order for how society is to function.

An irresponsible, over-inflated welfare system promotes laziness.

Extortion and Corruption

There are unrighteous attitudes that hinder kingdom economics, and there are also unrighteous laws and practices. Repeatedly, God condemns the personal and systemic evil of governments that keep people poor, oppressed, needy, and disenfranchised. It is a primary role of civil government to identify and root out this evil so people are not denied the opportunity to be productive and escape poverty. Nehemiah 5 records a case of extortion among the Jews who came back under this great leader. The people cried out to Nehemiah for relief because they were being mistreated economically.

Some of the people were just plain poor (Neh. 5:2). Others were losing ownership of their property because they had to mortgage it to buy food (v. 3). Still others were having to borrow money to pay their taxes (v. 4). Worst of all, some of God's people were being sold into slavery to pay their bills (v. 5), which meant they could leave no legacy to their children.

When Nehemiah heard all of this, he got angry because he discovered that "the nobles and the rulers" (government officials, v. 7) were extorting money from their fellow Jews. Those in power were ripping off their own people because they had the power and position to do so. They were charging the people heavy interest rates to borrow the money they needed to live.

In other words, systems were in place to make sure all the money went to those at the top. None of it was filtering down. People could borrow money, but they had to sell their children into slavery to do it. This was systemic economic injustice, which is evil at its core because God curses ungodly structures (Prov. 13:23), and because it robs people of the fruit of their labor. Such injustice must be challenged precisely as Nehemiah, a righteous political leader, challenged it.

Notice what he did. He called for a march (v. 7, "great assembly"), addressed the spiritual issues involved (vv. 8–9), and set up a system of restitution (vv. 10–13). The result was the restoration of justice and a renewed opportunity for people to benefit from their labor. In addition, a mountain of debt was removed in one day.

God hates unjust systems and practices. He made His view clear in James 5:1–6, which speaks to the unjust employer who withheld his workers' wages because he was only interested in his own profits.

Economic injustice can also be built into a governmental system that then prevents people from reaping and enjoying the maximum fruit of their labor, which is God's gift to mankind (Eccl. 2:24; 3:13;

5:18–19). Communism, socialism, and other Marxist social and economic ideologies are systems that establish a hierarchy in which the leaders inform the citizens that they will work for the state and only get from their work what the government decides for them.

This is one reason that communist and socialist regimes ultimately cannot stand without greatly limiting or denying freedom. Of course, the bigger reason these regimes fail is that they deny or reduce God's existence and try to rule Him and His principles out of life. This includes seeking to muzzle the role of the church and limit religious freedom. However, even capitalism, when it permits greedy monopolies to be built with unjust wages and labor laws, reflects another form of economic injustice.

Unjust Taxation

Another hindrance to God's economic agenda occurs when a government overtaxes its people, resulting in state-sanctioned theft. We are talking about democratic and republic governments here as well as socialist and communist governments. Whenever the government overtaxes its citizens, it commits a systemic evil. When Israel first demanded a king, Samuel warned the people that if they got a king, he would take the best of their produce for his court and impose heavy taxes on them (1 Sam. 8:10–18; 1 Kings 21:1–19). High taxation, then, is an indication of divine judgment and rejection of God's sovereign rule and covenantal structure.

Whenever the government overtaxes its citizens, it commits a systemic evil.

Samuel was saying that the king (i.e., government) would demand more of the people than they were obligated to give to God Himself. God required 10 percent, the tithe, as the basic financial obligation for His people. The king would demand more than that, Samuel told the Israelites. He was saying that no government should demand more from its people than the person who owns it all, who is God.

It is also unthinkable for the government to steal a family's wealth through an inheritance tax or to tax its citizens for property they own. We in America are under that evil, but it is also partly our fault. We have asked the government to do things that government was never meant to do, and the government is charging us for those services at a much higher rate than would be necessary if we were properly decentralized. The Bible promotes a free market economic system, since rulers are prohibited from confiscating property owned by individuals (1 Sam. 8:11–17). Civil government is to protect freedom (Lev. 25:10).

Because Christians have robbed God of His tithe, we are paying much more than that amount (up to nearly 40 percent) in unjust taxation as God's judgment on our spiritual theft. Once we ask the government to take over things like charity, medical care, and education, government is going to tax us excessively to pay for all those systems. And when government begins performing illegitimate functions, it becomes spiritually bankrupt, leading to excessive deficit spending and out-of-control debt—because remember, economics is a spiritual issue.

Keep in mind, I'm not saying that Scripture indicates taxation is wrong. In fact, it is right for civil government to collect taxes for the divinely authorized kingdom role it is given to fulfill (Rom. 13:6–7). But Scripture does not support a progressive tax where arbitrary standards and self-interest are used to assess tax percentages. The higher the tax rate the less economic freedom a person has, and the less resources that are available to encourage businesses to invest and grow, resulting in greater opportunity for employment and growth in income. The result is also increasing dependency on the state.

Rather, the Bible recognizes a flat tax where all pay the same assigned percentage, which of necessity means the rich pay more based on an objective standard. Such a flat tax illustrated by the tithe also serves to limit the size of government. Also, individuals should only be taxed on 90 percent of their income if they use 10 percent for charity. This will incentivize giving in the private sector to meet human needs. A flat tax is the only objective way of measuring a person or a company's fair share as opposed to the subjective whims of bureaucrats. All other taxes should be based on consumption, not on property ownership.

Since God's kingdom is decentralized and operates from the bottom up, the best way to manage taxation is for states to tax their citizens an income tax and then the federal government taxes the states for the divinely authorized scope of the responsibilities it has been assigned by God. Unjust taxation stems from an unbiblical view of life. It is another form of theft.

Taxation provides the opportunity for the civil government to support the society, but when it is done according to unbiblical methods, it leads to corruption, destruction, and inefficiency. It also opens the door for misuse. Health care is one of the areas where misuse can take place. Health care should be driven by a robust free market economy, not an overblown bureaucracy. This includes allowing insurance companies to compete across state lines. It means allowing qualified groups not just related to employment to receive group coverage. It means requiring all family units to have at a minimum coverage for catastrophic illnesses or accidents.

Finally, it means putting all currently uninsured people who have preexisting catastrophic illnesses into a separate pool funded by the government so that insurance companies no longer have that as an economic concern. This or similar ideas will automatically lower cost, expand coverage, and limit the federal government bureaucratic involvement in health care, while simultaneously placing the burden for health care on the individual and the family, where it belongs. Of course, the government should provide high-quality health care coverage for those who are the responsible poor (i.e., those who seek to maximize opportunities to become productive yet fall short of what is needed to survive).

BUILDING FOR TODAY
WHILE INVESTING FOR TOMORROW

Here is an important item on the agenda of kingdom economic development. We need to prepare for life, because we might be here for a while. There's a great example of this in Jeremiah 29:4–7. The Jews were exiles in Babylon. A false prophet had come and told the people that they would be out of there and back home within two years (Jer. 28:11), so they didn't need to worry about any economic issues.

Ownership always requires some sort of investment.

But God had a different message. He told Jeremiah to tell the people, "Build houses and live in them; and plant gardens, and eat their produce" (29:5). In other words, start economic development, because you are going to be here a long time. Don't sit back and depend on government charity to take care of you when you retire.

Building houses and planting vineyards suggests ownership, a key element of a kingdom economic strategy. And ownership always requires some sort of investment. God told them that while they were waiting for a better tomorrow, they were to work in the day they were in.

Do you know why so many of us kingdom citizens are in debt up to our ears? Because we have listened to the culture teaching us to spend while we have ignored God teaching us to invest. In Luke 19:11–27, Jesus told a classic parable of the need to invest for the future. The master in the parable gave each of his slaves a different amount of money and told them to invest it so that they would have a profit when he returned.

Many of us would have spent the money we got if that happened to us. It would have been gone, because we do not understand that God does not give us money just to spend but also to invest.

Before commercial seed became widely available, a farmer who ate all his crops would not have any crops the next year. He always left some seeds to put back into the ground so he would have new crops the next year. You and I must invest if we are going to be a kingdom-oriented people. Our government must learn to do the same.

There is no such thing, by the way, as equality of outcomes (i.e., equity). While people are all born with equal value, they are also born with different levels of talent, different degrees of motivation, and in different situations that offer different amounts of opportunity. But there is such a thing as maximizing what God has given us.

Nehemiah 11:1–2 is a good example of what I'm talking about. After the walls of Jerusalem were rebuilt, Nehemiah got the people to invest in the future of their community:

> The leaders of the people lived in Jerusalem, but the rest of the people cast lots to bring one out of ten to live in Jerusalem, the holy city, while nine-tenths remained in the other cities. And the people blessed all the men who volunteered to live in Jerusalem.

Nehemiah brought people from the suburbs back into Jerusalem so they could invest in the community and build it up. Before, there were no walls, no businesses, no community—just chaos. By getting the people to invest in their own future, Nehemiah raised the standards of the community.

And when you raise the standards and incentivize investments (i.e., banning race redlining), everything in a community goes up with it. Property values go up because the businesses go up, and job opportunities increase. There is stability in the community. We have

GDOM POLITICS

the power to do that in our communities as well if we would get serious about fulfilling the economic agenda of God's kingdom.

Civil government should offer economic incentives for businesses to develop or expand to depressed or impoverished areas in order to provide opportunities for personal, familial, and community development, since special focus is to be given to serving the poor, oppressed, widows, and orphans (Lev. 19:9–10; Deut. 24:17–22). It is evil and satanic for civic government to seek to control free trade (Rev. 13:16–17).

I gave a kingdom challenge to our church in relation to economics. I'd like to share it with you.

You may have grown up in an impoverished area and now you are in the suburbs. Maybe you have a nice house, two cars, and good clothes, which you don't need to apologize for if you earned those possessions and are using them legitimately. We must ask ourselves two questions.

First, *has the blessing of God on us become a blessing to others?* If not, we are not living by a kingdom economic agenda, and God's blessing can become a curse. It has already become a curse for some of us because we are in an economic prison called deep debt, or have allowed the pursuit of mammon to destroy our spiritual lives, reputations, and families. Some of us are only one paycheck away from going back to the impoverished area.

Second, *do we have inner peace?* If the resources we have come from God, He always gives joy with it (Prov. 10:22).

We need to get on God's economic agenda in our personal and family lives. Our churches and communities need to get on God's agenda based on the absolute authority of His Word. We need to believe that the earth is the Lord's and live in light of that truth.

God has a kingdom perspective on economics, and if we would return to it, we would see God's hand in the culture and society transforming our communities and restoring our strength as a nation.

Civil government operating properly under God's kingdom economic agenda should both promote and protect the free and just exchange of goods and services, which naturally results in the growth of capital and the economic benefit to the citizens. This means removing dishonest gain from the marketplace (Ex. 18:21).

When God's economic principles are properly implemented, people are enabled to exercise their creativity, initiative, and responsibilities for productively using the earth's resources to benefit themselves, as well as others. A just, righteous, and free economic system appropriately encourages and empowers all people, including the poor and oppressed, to maximize their productive potential.

PART THREE

The Citizens
of Kingdom
Politics

Chapter 9

THE LEADERSHIP OF KINGDOM CITIZENS

One day a train conductor was moving throughout the train in order to take up the tickets from the passengers. He came to the first passenger and took his ticket. Yet when he looked at the ticket, he hesitated. Then he said, "Excuse me, sir, but I think you are on the wrong train. Your ticket is for a train headed in another direction."

That's when the passenger replied, "Well, I'm confused because I went to the ticket agent, and he told me that this was the train I was supposed to take for where I was supposed to go."

This further confounded the train conductor, who decided to step off the train before it left to go speak to the ticket agent about the train he had told the passenger to board. When the train conductor explained to the ticket agent that he had put the gentleman on the wrong train, the ticket agent responded with a surprising reply. "Actually, no I didn't," he said. Then added, "You are on the wrong train."

The train conductor had boarded the wrong train. And when the person who should know what is going on and where a train is headed is lost, then we shouldn't be surprised that everyone else on the train winds up confused as well. When it comes to our world, and our nation in particular, much of our destination is tied to those who should know where we need to go. It is tied to the quality of politicians who have made it their goal to lead in our land. It is tied to the civic leaders who have been given the responsibility within the various levels of government to provide a direction that will facilitate the conditions for a well-ordered civil society. Scripture is clear that when legitimate, responsible political leadership is absent, a society and its citizens descend into chaos (Judg. 17:6; 21:25).

Leadership is a fundamental feature of kingdom governance. Political leadership will often show up in the policies politicians support and what they spend the majority of their time focusing on. But in addition to how a politician votes or a civic leader presents or supports various legislation, we should also be concerned with the person as well.

In God's kingdom, having the right person with the right policies packaged together is how a culture and a country progresses well. Yet when the two become disconnected because you have the wrong policies or the wrong people then you have set up the nation for an increase in conflict, confusion, and even regression on a global scale.

That's why it is so important to look for the right people of high character and kingdom perspective to represent us as politicians and civic leaders. When we examine who to put in office or who to support through our time, donations, or our vote, we need to look at the policies they support and whether those policies will achieve the goal of maintaining a safe, just, righteous, and compassionately responsible environment for freedom to flourish. And while we have a say in how politicians are able to serve and in what capacity, we also need to remember that the Bible makes it clear that when it comes to God, He determines the outcome. Proverbs 8:15–16 says, "By me kings reign, and rulers decree justice. By me princes rule, and nobles, all who judge rightly." God orchestrates who the rulers are, ultimately, because government is His institution. This is why God instructed leaders to humbly seek Him and His Word for how to govern people properly (Deut. 17:18–20). The most important thing a political leader can do is establish and encourage citizens to operate by a biblical standard.

In fact, in Romans 13 political and civic leaders are often referred to as "deacons." They are called "ministers of God" three times in the first seven verses alone. Keep in mind, this is the case when talking about the Roman government. They are not talking about the Christian government or leadership. It is the secular society that is referenced in Romans 13. God frequently refers to civic leaders as His servants. They are His ministers who are to reflect His rule in the land.

Thus, the closer a civic leader is to the character and competence of God, as well as to the governing guidelines of God, the more ordered the society will be. Conversely, the further the leaders are in their character and competence with regard to biblical policy, the further that nation will be from God and His divine order for society. That also means there will exist more confusion in the land. Recognizing God means more than just using His name, saying prayers, and randomly quoting Bible verses in political speeches. It means allowing His worldview to influence and affect policy.

Throughout Scripture we read about God choosing civic leaders to raise up, as well as civic leaders to tear down (Isa. 45:1–5). He is constantly manipulating the leadership process for good or for judgment. Oftentimes the judgment comes as a result of the hearts of the people—the citizens—having turned away from God. When this takes place to such a degree as is frequent in today's culture, God allows wicked or evil leadership to assume governing positions. In this way, His judgment is released on the nation as an attempt to draw people to repentance and reignite a heart for Him in the collective culture at large.

Proverbs 29:2 states it this way, "When the righteous increase, the people rejoice, but when a wicked man rules, people groan." When the leadership is evil and corrupt, then the legislation will not achieve its biblical goals, and citizens, as well as society at large, will suffer.

Looking at many of our elected leaders today, it might be easy to forget that the system of government belongs to God. But regardless of what we see reflected in our civic leadership's character and policies, we must align ourselves with a biblically correct view of politics. In order to do so, let me explain theologically how the principle of leadership works in God's governing process. Because just as a church can have a group of poor-performing deacons or even a group of high-performing and quality deacons, there can be poor-performing ministers of government and high-performing and quality ministers of government. These qualifications are predicated on how these individuals view their roles and seek to uphold their roles as policymakers.

COVENANT-BASED LEADERSHIP QUALIFICATIONS

To understand why this is so critical, we must revisit the principle of the covenant. God operates His world through covenants. As a reminder, a covenant is a legally binding relationship that has been established by God. The more you operate or function in sync with God and His rules, whether as a leader or even as a culture, the more you will progress in society.

A covenant is like a football on a football field. Everything must be properly aligned to the football. If something is not properly aligned—for example, players setting up ahead of where the football is on the field—it is a foul. Depending on what team the player is on, it could be called as being "offsides," or as "encroachment." Similarly, if a player fails to handle a football properly and he drops it, it becomes a fumble. When the football hits the plain of the goal line, it signals a touchdown. When a football goes through the uprights, it becomes a field goal. In other words, everything depends on where everything else is in relationship to the football. Likewise, in God's kingdom, everything depends on where everything else is in relationship to the covenant.

This is true of the family. It is true of the church. It is also true of institutions. The government falls into this arena of institutions, and by God's common grace, He has provided the opportunity for all people and nations to benefit from His instruction, orientation, and commands. Thus, just as a football determines whether a team or player is in alignment with the rules of the grid-iron, how civic leaders function, both in private and in public, determines whether or not a nation is in alignment with the rules of God.

Because of this close tie between God's favor or judgment and the behavior, character, and policies of civic leaders, it is critical that we seek leaders who are in alignment with God. Scripture tells us in Daniel 2:21 that the success of civic leaders depends on God and what He supplies them by way of wisdom. We read, "It is He who changes the times and the epochs; He removes kings and establishes kings; He gives wisdom to wise men and knowledge to men of understanding." God determines the successes, or failures, of leaders. And He does so based on the rules of His covenant.

That's why we cannot talk about government or politics without talking about God and His role regarding civic leaders. The principle of representation, which is what a civic leader assumes when elected, is a key element to a biblical covenant. This means that in God's covenantal hierarchical order, the one who is legitimately and functionally above you also represents you. This is why God calls husbands to submit to legitimate spiritual authority (Titus 2:1, 6), wives to submit to the legitimate authority of their husbands (Eph. 5:22–24), church members to submit to the legitimate authority of church leadership (Heb. 13:17), and citizens to submit to the legitimate authority of civil government (1 Peter 2:13).

When a civic leader represents you because he or she represents your district, city, county, school, state, or nation, they make decisions on your behalf. You no longer have a say in these decisions legislatively once you turn over government representation to an elected leader. For example, if the president or Congress says we are going to war, you cannot say that we aren't. Yes, you may protest their decision, but their decision is still the decision that stands. You may not have voted to go to war yourself, but because your elected leader represents you, the decision to go to war is made for you.

> **Leadership is critical. Poor leadership leaves lasting repercussions.**

America exists as a representative system wherein we elect civic leaders to reflect our values in the land. These civic leaders represent us on behalf of the nation. That's how God set up government to work—representatively. He also sets up families to work that way too wherein the father or the husband represents the family spiritually before God (1 Cor. 11:3; Gen. 18:19; Ex. 34:23–24). Similarly, spiritual leadership in a church represents the congregation before God (Heb. 13:17). Yet just because God established representatives in all these spheres of life does not mean that they carry out their roles well. That is why it is so important to pray for those in representative roles over you because if and when they provoke God's judgment, oftentimes that judgment will spill over to those they represent as well. The Israelites, for example, failed to enter the promised land due to the unrighteous decision and influence of their male representatives (Num. 13:25–33).

Leadership is critical. Poor leadership leaves lasting repercussions. Just look at Adam, for example. Romans 5 tells us that "in Adam all died." The reason why all of humanity has been placed on a pathway of physical death and separation from God is due to Adam. Our initial representative before God chose to disobey God and as a result ushered in the consequences we all continue to experience even now.

Because Adam failed in his role of representing the human race, he transferred to each of us the results of his failure. Adam should be an eye-opener for all of us on why it is so critical to choose our representatives wisely.

On the other hand, we have a representative, Jesus Christ, who did not fail. Jesus perfectly satisfied in His person and in His application of biblical truth both the will and the word of God. When someone accepts Jesus Christ as their personal sin-bearer and representative before God, they receive the benefits that Jesus secured on the cross. Representatives matter greatly. We should never hold this concept of voting or supporting political or civic candidates lightly, because once they are securely in place, we all fall under either the benefits or the consequences of their character and choices.

Understanding politics through a kingdom worldview is critical for every citizen. Far too many people fail to comprehend the covenantal connection between civic representatives and God, and thus fail to participate in the process of choosing these leaders wisely. God desires to bless the nations whose leaders follow His rule. He has made it perfectly clear on how a nation and its inhabitants are to secure the blessings they desire. He has not hidden His ways from us or kept the path to His benefits a secret. Deuteronomy 29:9 states it like this, "So keep the words of this covenant to do them, that you may prosper in all that you do."

If you want to truly pray "God bless America" and see the results of that prayer, then you need to make sure the leadership in our land are positioned to be recipients of the blessings of God in all they do and say. As our representatives, they serve as a transfer of either God's favor or a transfer of His judgment to the citizenry.

THE NEED FOR RESPONSIBLE LEADERS

Influencing the political nature of a nation involves influencing what people are put into power, not only for their policies but also for their character and personal qualities as well. Blessings flow through the biblio-centric principle of representation when the representatives choose to operate in covenant with God. That's just the way it is. Each of us has a responsibility to engage in politics at some level, and to let our voice and values be made known. We have this responsibility because each of us will experience the blessing or judgment transferred to us through our political representatives.

Unfortunately, many Christians will talk about agreement with a politician's policy while at the same time skip dealing with them as a person. But under God's covenantal plan, character and decision-making go hand in hand. If our representatives are going to successfully establish a funnel through which God's blessings will flow, they must focus both on policy and on their own personal values.

The book of Exodus tells us the kinds of leaders we are to look for and endorse when choosing or supporting our civic leadership. There exist certain qualifications that will be helpful in promoting God's blessings in the land. We read about some of them in Exodus 18:21 where it says,

> "Furthermore, you shall select out of all the people able men who fear God, men of truth, those who hate dishonest gain; and you shall place these over them as leaders of thousands, of hundreds, of fifties and of tens."

Based on this passage, we are, first of all, to look for leaders who fear God. These are leaders who take God seriously. A leader who fears God refers to someone who not only believes in God but who also seeks to find out what God says on a subject in order to implement His will in a matter at hand. Someone who fears God will actively seek out God's perspective. Fearing God does not mean referencing God's name at a breakfast or banquet or while campaigning. Nor does it mean saying, "God bless America." Fearing God shows up when a politician brings God's viewpoint to bear in terms of the actions or policies and legislation at hand. A politician who fears God takes God seriously.

Maybe it'll help me explain this concept of fearing God if I compare it to electricity. You need to take electricity seriously because it can benefit you greatly when you do. On the other hand, if you choose to put a screwdriver in a live socket, the electricity will wind up hurting you. You must take electricity seriously, and even fear the power of electricity, if you are to access the benefits of electricity while simultaneously avoiding the dangers of it.

When a nation has leaders who do not take God seriously, the help the nation should be getting from heaven through them and to the people becomes a curse on the land instead. In the Bible we read about many lands that were cursed because the leadership refused to fear God and take Him seriously. As Christians, we need to make sure that our representative leadership is held accountable to God's will and His ways. As Psalm 2:10 puts it, "Now therefore, O kings, show discernment; take warning, O judges of the earth." Government leaders are expected to govern based on God's standards (Prov. 8:15).

When a leader fails to fear God, God can bring that leader down, as well as bring down the people under their care who supported them. One of the greatest biblical illustrations of that is Nebuchadnezzar. We read about him in the book of Daniel. King Nebuchadnezzar ruled with great power. He ruled so easily and for so long that it wound up going to his head. He thought there was more to him than there actually was. We see this in Daniel 4:4 where it says, "I, Nebuchadnezzar, was at ease in my house and flourishing in my palace."

One day, King Nebuchadnezzar did more than just "flourish in his palace." This time he stood out on his portico in the shade and said, "Is this not Babylon the great, which I myself have built as a royal residence by the might of my power and for the glory of my majesty?" (v. 30b). Essentially, he stood there with his chest out and proclaimed, "I am the man!" He was narcissistic to the max. In fact, he thought the entire world revolved around him for the glory of his own majesty. That's when God decided to help him out a bit and get him to see reality once again. Because even though the king was over a great kingdom, there was Someone who was still over him: God.

When the state and its leadership develop a Theo-ego (a God complex) and seek to overstep its bounds by rejecting God's guidelines for civil government, then Christians have the right and responsibility to righteously and peacefully protest. Scripture is full of protests and resistance to unrighteous laws when leaders overstep their boundaries. For example:

Jochebed and the Hebrew midwives rejected Pharaoh's edicts of infanticide. (Ex. 1:15–2:4)

Rahab was subversive in Jericho. (Heb. 11:31; Josh. 2:1–21)

Shadrack, Meshack, and Abednego rejected the requirement to bow to the state's idolatrous demands. (Dan. 3:1–18)

Daniel rejected and disobeyed the infringement on his religious freedom. (Dan. 6:1–15)

Peter and John disobeyed the mandate to deny them freedom of speech and religion. (Acts 4:13–20; 5:18–29)

Paul instituted the first Christian "sit in" when he was illegally arrested and beaten. (Acts 16:22–40)

As you can see, there are a number of examples of righteous protest to unrighteous laws. Both within and outside of the political systems, believers are to appropriately make their voices of righteous protest heard.

God had shown Nebuchadnezzar what would happen to him if he got a big head earlier in a dream. He had shown him through a godly politician named Daniel. Daniel served in this secular government, which is a great example to all of us how Christians can serve in politics and make an impact for good. When the king had a terrifying dream that he could not interpret, he had called on Daniel to interpret it for him. This is what God was showing the king in his dream. It was given as a warning. We read,

> "This is the interpretation, O king, and this is the decree of the Most High, which has come upon my lord the king: that you be driven away from mankind and your dwelling place be with the beasts of the field, and you be given grass to eat like cattle and be drenched with the dew of heaven; and seven periods of time will pass over you, until you recognize that the Most High is ruler over the realm of mankind and bestows it on whomever He wishes. And in that it was commanded to leave the stump with the roots of the tree, your kingdom will be assured to you after you recognize that it is Heaven that rules. Therefore, O king, may my advice be pleasing to you: break away now from your sins by doing righteousness and from your iniquities by showing mercy to the poor, in case there may be a prolonging of your prosperity." (Dan. 4:24–27)

Nebuchadnezzar did not understand his role under God. The king, or politician, who fails to understand his place, as powerful or talented as he or she may be, can expect to be shown their place under God at some point. This is what happened to Herod when God took his life because he received worship that belonged to God alone. What was equally as bad was when people looked to this governmental leader as the ultimate source for life, liberty, and security

(Acts 12:22–23). Political leaders only have delegated authority. They are not to be worshiped.

Immediately after Nebuchadnezzar made his contentious claim of his own great power, God let the dream in which He had warned him play out. Daniel 4:33 says,

> Immediately the word concerning Nebuchadnezzar was fulfilled; and he was driven away from mankind and began eating grass like cattle, and his body was drenched with the dew of heaven until his hair had grown like eagles' feathers and his nails like birds' claws.

Nebuchadnezzar didn't fall due to his policies or his ruling power. He fell due to his pride. And while we shouldn't skip the examination of a person's policies, we must also hold their character in high esteem.

We are to affirm those leaders who lead us with humility and honesty. But the passage we looked at earlier says the second quality we should look for in civic leaders is that of affirming truth. Civic leaders must be men and women of truth. That means they must also protect integrity. Now, that doesn't mean they are perfect. You and I will never find a perfect leader simply because leaders are human. But when you look at who to support as civic leaders, you want to find someone whose goal it is to be honest, defend truth, and live with integrity along with high ethical standards.

INTEGRITY IN LEADERSHIP ROLES

Have you ever been behind a car that is signaling right but turning left? That's a dangerous place to be. The person driving the car has their signal on, telling you they are going to turn one way, but they wind up turning the opposite way. This is dangerous because the other drivers around this confused driver make their decisions based on what he or she has indicated. If someone chooses to pass the driver on the left because they are signaling to turn right, but then they turn left, both vehicles may wind up in an accident.

Signaling truthfully is an important part of driving safely. Similarly, political leaders must be people of truth. They must be people who can be trusted to do what they say they will do. They cannot be people who intentionally seek to deceive others, or they will only create confusion and chaos, and even danger, in the land. More and more these days, truth is under fire. I preached an entire sermon series on the subject of truth not too long ago because it is a kingdom value that, if it dies, our entire society will die with it. Everyone needs to return to the truth, not just politicians and civic leaders. We are witnessing the demise of a nation due to the devolution of this kingdom value called truth.

God does not want a fake politician running things. He wants people of character, like Daniel, who, when the civic leaders of his day sought to oust him because they were jealous of his position of influence, they could find nothing wrong with his policies or his person. The first ten verses of Daniel 6 speak to Daniel's extraordinary character and work as a politician in a secular society. Daniel distinguished himself to such a degree that those who tried to trip him up could find no reason to condemn him. So they had to invent a reason and then trap him in it.

God wants you and me to support politicians who have integrity, coupled with a biblical, kingdom-minded worldview like Daniel's. We ought to look for the highest caliber of people who will function according to His covenantal rules so that He can pour out His blessing on the land.

We've seen that civic leaders should be people who fear God by taking Him and His word seriously. We've also seen that they are to be people of truth. Lastly, in the passage we looked at earlier, we read that politicians are to be known as "able men." That is a phrase to indicate that they are productive. This refers to both men and women who function in an excellent manner at the highest possible level. God doesn't want civic leaders just trying to get by each day and put in as little work as possible. He wants civic leaders who are willing to give their best on behalf of society.

Civic leaders are to represent a standard of excellence to everyone else. Now, we understand this standard when it comes to our medical care or our doctors. No one wants a mediocre doctor. Neither does anyone want mediocre or ill-prepared food service. I don't know about you, but I wouldn't want a mediocre pilot. We have standards when it comes to certain areas of our lives, so why shouldn't we have standards when it comes to our civic leaders?

We are to support able men and women who serve productively and with integrity, and who do not seek to rob others based on their positions of power. They should not be lazy or self-serving. They should be people who follow the principle set for us in Ecclesiastes 9:10, which says, "Whatever your hand finds to do, do it with all your might." Civic leaders are not to serve with sloth. They are not to serve just to get a paycheck. We must look for and support men and women who work hard at their jobs, who do not settle simply to get it over with.

We also read in the passage above that they must be selfless servants. They are to "hate dishonest gain." In other words, they work on behalf of the betterment of the people. It is not, first and foremost, for the betterment of themselves. They are not to create policies that steal from those they serve through undermining them, or through taking a cut under the table to decide for something that is not in the favor of the people. Civic leaders ought to be people who can be trusted to do what is right, effective, and honest.

Kingdom-minded politicians and civic leaders ought to be about the good of society, based on biblical values and principles. They are to help people discover greater ways of living responsibly in order to maximize the life and talents God has given them. The people who are represented by the civic leaders should be better off because of the service of their political representatives, and not worse off due to their desire for power or position.

We live in a day when far too many people crave celebrity status. Everybody wants their fifteen minutes of fame. Everyone wants to be recognized and applauded. But too often that comes at the cost of putting the focus on themselves and not on those they are there to serve. We should seek to raise up leaders who desire to be recognized for the kind of service they supply to people.

When we have representative leaders over us who we didn't vote into office or support in any way, and yet they now serve over us as governing officials, one of the things we can do is pray for them. Scripture says, in 1 Timothy 2:1–2, that we are to pray for all those who lead us, including our political leaders. This includes the president, vice-president, congressmen and women, city council members, mayors, governors, senators, or anyone in leadership. You and I are to pray for them. It is amazing to me how many people will criticize a politician who they are unwilling to pray for. If we could muster more prayer than criticism, we will experience more positive action.

One of the reasons we are to pray for them is because God calls us to submit to the leaders above us. We read in 1 Peter 2:13–14,

> Submit yourselves for the Lord's sake to every human institution, whether to a king as the one in authority, or to governors as sent by him for the punishment of evildoers and the praise of those who do right.

Because we are instructed to submit to leadership established in human institutions, we need to be careful to elect leadership that has our best interests in mind. And when that is not possible, we need to be proactive about praying for the existing leadership so that their hearts will turn toward God. This passage doesn't say we have to like the leadership placed over us, but we do need to submit to them and pray for them and their leadership. Most importantly, we are not to bad-mouth them but respect their position (1 Peter 2:17). Exodus 22:28 puts it like this: "You shall not curse God, nor curse a ruler of your people."

We need greater civility toward our civic leaders in our culture. Everyone feels free to put anyone and everyone down in some of the worst ways possible. Yet Paul reflected how we are to speak of the leaders over us when he referred to Nero as his deacon. Nero ruled over Rome. You couldn't get much worse than Nero when it came to rulers. He was a terrible "deacon," yet Paul still respected the office, even if he didn't like the person in the office. Ecclesiastes 10:20 states it like this,

> Furthermore, in your bedchamber do not curse a king, and in your sleeping rooms do not curse a rich man, for a bird of the heavens will carry the sound and the winged creature will make the matter known.

You are not to speak badly of the leaders placed over you, even in private when you think nobody is listening. To "curse" in the context of this passage means to wish evil on someone. It is not talking about saying swear words. We are not to do that because it insults God, since God has chosen for this leader to rule at this time, even if that choice is for judgment. As long as the person is in office, you drive away God's intervention and blessing when you choose to curse or belittle them with your words and wishes because you do not like them.

God commands us not to do this. If and when we approach leaders we disagree with, in order to point out our disagreements with them, we are to do it in an honorable fashion. We need to do it with self-control and respect, like how Paul spoke to Felix when he appeared before him in Acts 24:25. Paul told Felix the truth about how he felt and the things he felt Felix was doing wrong, but he did it in a way that allowed Felix to listen because it was said with respect. Leaders are to be challenged about their moral character (Matt. 14:3–4; Mark 6:18; Luke 3:18–19).

The Bible is clear that we are to respect authority (Prov. 24:21). We are to honor them and pray for them. We are to condemn any wrong that they do, but we should do it in a way that is honorable and respectful, all while praying for a change of character. After all, God changed a lot of people's character in Scripture over the years. Moses was a murderer. Peter denied Jesus. Solomon was a womanizer. Mary Magdalene was a loose woman. There are people all throughout Scripture that, when God got ahold of their hearts, he fixed their character and gave them a new start. Just like He did with King Nebuchadnezzar.

Seven years after Nebuchadnezzar lost his mind as a result of his pride, he was able to come to himself and his reason returned to him. He got his sanity back because he had been humbled. In fact, he went on to bless God and give God the glory and praise that was due His name for all the power God had shown in establishing his governance (Dan. 4:34–37).

This man changed due to the impact of a righteous politician speaking into his life—Daniel. He was able to come to a place of humility and truth as a political leader because of Daniel's involvement in his life and God's allowing of circumstances to teach him what is real. This also resulted in a change in legislation. We need to learn from this situation. Rather than criticize our civic leaders in an unbiblical way—we need to pray for them. We need to encourage them to look to God. We need to ask God to intervene in their lives. Scripture has examples of political leaders who He restored to political leadership when they repented (1 Chron. 33:1–20; Jonah 3:1–10).

When you and I make a decision on who to support politically—whether in a vote, donation, or any other manner, we have to look at both the person and the policy. Ideally, you want good in both. You want great people with great policies who will run the government. But oftentimes—in fact, most of the time—you don't get both. And sometimes you don't get either. In these situations, we have to make a choice. When presented with options that are not consistent with God's definition of government, what should a person do? You need to examine your conscience and find the one who most aligns with your conscience under God. Because each of us has different backgrounds, experiences, and levels of growth as Christians—people are going to choose differently. But whatever way you choose, you need to stand for the King of kings and Lord of lords and the unity of His church. We ought never allow a demonic political divide to simultaneously divide the people of God.

Ultimately, we have a representative in the Lord Jesus Christ, and it is under Him that we are to live and align ourselves. He calls us to love one another and pursue the unity of the faith. If someone supports a different person than you do, then pray for them. Or talk to them. Listen to them as to why. You may have something to learn. If, after all of that, you still disagree, then seek to come together and stay together on what remains our common ground in the faith—the ministry and governance of Jesus Christ and His kingdom agenda over all.

Chapter 10

THE VOTING OF KINGDOM CITIZENS

One of the most important ways to bring God's view into politics and the policies of a nation is through your own voice. I know of no other simpler and more straightforward way to let your voice count than to participate in politics through your vote. Your vote is your voice.

Many, if not most, Christians begin with the wrong question of *who they should vote for* rather than the more important question of *how they should vote*. Asking the correct question is fundamental to knowing how to arrive at the correct answer.

As a kingdom citizen, you are to be a kingdom voter. Kingdom voting is *the opportunity and responsibility of committed Christians to partner with God by expanding His rule in society through civil government*. It is only to the degree that you include God's person and God's policies in politics that you witness His presence and His power in society. When we involve God in politics, we can begin to see healing in the church so that it can then be modeled in the culture.

Voting is your opportunity to engage in politics in a meaningful way. I call it an opportunity because not every culture offers this option to its people. Not every country allows its citizens to vote on its leadership. Voting is your responsibility. It is your partnership in the political process. Failure to take advantage of this privilege nullifies a person's right to legitimately complain about the direction of the government that they refuse to engage on political issues even at a minimal level. The government, on the other hand, should encourage and facilitate equal access to the ballot box for all qualified citizens and remove every vestige of voter suppression and gerrymandering.

> **Voting is your opportunity to engage in politics in a meaningful way.**

Throughout the Bible, God called on people to partner with Him. Scripture makes it clear that we work together with God (2 Cor. 6:1). Thus, while we must pray for God to bring healing to our land, we must also partner with God for this healing to take place. When our part of the partnership wanes and we fail to fulfill our responsibility, we don't change who God is, but we may alter how He chooses to work. God has established the process of partnership, through forms of voting, for our decision-making and engagement with culture, although He alone determines the ultimate outcome (Prov. 16:33; Acts 1:24–26).

If we are going to see God intervene and inject Himself in the affairs of a collapsing society and a devastated nation, then we need to return to Him. I'm not talking about returning to Him by simply throwing His name around or saying more public prayers. Rather, we must return to Him in a way that embraces His person and His policies at the level that He can then influence the culture. It is only then that we will experience His healing presence in our lives, churches, and in our nation.

The further God is removed from the life of an individual, from the definition of a family, or from the running of a church, the more chaotic those entities become. The more chaotic those entities become then influences the level of chaos in the culture. God is not a cute addendum we toss around so that we can feel spiritual. God longs to be intricately involved in all we do and say, and especially in the running of our nation.

The theme of the Bible is the glory of God through the expansion of His kingdom. God is concerned about one thing: that He be glorified and His kingdom expanded. Once you leave that, you've left the theme of the Bible. And once you've left the Bible, you've left God. The Bible is clear that God rules over all. Psalm 22:28 states it like this: "For dominion belongs to the LORD and He rules over the nations."

God is King. He is running a kingdom that involves the nations. God has established the world in such a way to give you the opportunity and responsibility to partici-

If you are a Christian and you name the name of Jesus Christ, you don't get to leave God out of your vote.

pate in the process of how He runs it. You participate, at a minimum, through your vote. Now, I understand that this creates consternation because what we are voting on is not God or His policies, but rather people to fill roles who may or may not reflect God's principles. But we are still called upon to vote according to our conscience in a manner that will seek to bring God glory.

If you are a Christian and you name the name of Jesus Christ, you don't get to leave God out of your vote. Nor do you just get to vote how you want to vote. You only get to vote for God's glory and the expansion of His kingdom. That's the primary drive behind your vote. Your vote should seek to expand God's kingdom rule on earth. And while I understand and acknowledge that there are a lot of variances in terms of specific applications to specific policies and politicians under that banner, the goal of glorifying God must be foremost in your vote. God's glory is magnified when He is recognized in His proper sovereign place over the nations.

This is why church leaders should give biblical answers to the issues facing their community and nation. They should challenge their membership to vote, as well as provide voter registration drives. They can even host political forums so people can hear from political candidates on how closely they are aligned to a kingdom worldview.

TAKING POLITICAL SIDES

In Joshua 5, we read about the battle of Jericho. God had already promised Joshua victory in this battle, but Joshua still had to partner with God in bringing this victory into history. God was going to give Joshua victory but only on His terms. In other words, if the walls of Jericho were going to fall, Joshua had to follow God in order for the walls to fall.

As we read about this partnership in the process of securing the victory over Jericho, we learn more about how God sets an example for us when it comes to politics. The story we are going to look at starts in verse 13 where we read,

> Now it came about when Joshua was by Jericho, that he lifted up his eyes and looked, and behold, a man was standing opposite him with his sword drawn in his hand, and Joshua went to him and said to him, "Are you for us or for our adversaries?" He said, "No; rather I indeed come now as captain of the host of the LORD." And Joshua fell on his face to the earth, and bowed down, and said to him, "What has my lord to say to his servant?" The captain of the LORD's host

said to Joshua, "Remove your sandals from your feet, for the place where you are standing is holy." And Joshua did so. (vv. 13–15)

In this passage, we find a man who is ready to fight. He is ready to go to battle. He has his sword drawn in his hand when Joshua runs into him. The obvious question comes from Joshua at this point, "Are you for us or for our enemy?" In other words, "Who's side are you on?"

This is a common question we hear when it comes to politics in America. Are you a Republican or a Democrat? Whose side are you on? Are you a liberal? Or are you a conservative? Are you a left-winger? Or are you a right-winger? It's a common question we hear today, and it is really no different than what Joshua wanted to know of the man holding the sword and standing in front of him. It matters what side someone is on, or at least we think it does. Joshua wanted to know where this man leaned so that he could figure out his strategy and approach in confronting Jericho. After all, he was holding a sword.

If anyone ever asks me if I am a Republican or a Democrat, I respond that I am neither. I am a kingdom independent.

But rather than take a side, the man told Joshua that he was on no one's side but God's. He was the captain of the host of the Lord. He hadn't come to take sides. He had come operating on a whole other level. He was representing a whole other program. Joshua came from the chosen people and the chosen nation, but that didn't equate to God taking sides. Just because they were His chosen people didn't mean God automatically took their side. Nor was He on Jericho's side, a city of people who barely knew His name. Rather, God is a kingdom independent. Let me write that again in case you missed it: the God of the Bible is a kingdom independent. He doesn't take sides when it comes to doing battle. He sits as the King over all and it is His glory and His kingdom He seeks to expand.

God is on His own side. Because of this, if anyone ever asks me if I am a Republican or a Democrat, I respond that I am neither. I am a kingdom independent. In fact, I would encourage all Christians to view themselves as kingdom independents. A kingdom independent is *a Christian whose ultimate political alliance is to those persons, policies, and platforms that best represent the values of the kingdom of God.* Now, that may manifest itself as either a vote for a Republican candidate or a Democrat candidate, or you may vote as a libertarian, or even as a write-in, but the only absolute alignment there should be is with God and His kingdom perspective.

I'm sure you know about the soft drinks that don't have much sugar. They'll put the word *light* at the end of the name brand. A similar thing could be said for kingdom independents who either lean Republican or Democrat. At most, that person could be Republican-light or Democrat-light. This is because as a believer in Jesus Christ and as His disciple, you belong to another king and another kingdom. You are not to come and take sides. Rather, you are to usher in the full actualization of God's presence over all. God rules the nations. That means He is the One who calls the shots. He is the One who will have the last word. He is the One to determine how things should work out, not your political affiliation.

VOTING AS A KINGDOM INDEPENDENT

The God of the Bible does not ride on the backs of donkeys or elephants. The God of the Bible is His own independent. He only votes for Himself. Problems arise when it comes to our decisions regarding voting when there exists no political party that only votes God's way. Some represent God's priorities on certain things but not on others.

And vice versa. Thus, when it comes time to vote, one person may vote Republican because they are voting with an emphasis on life in the womb. But others may vote Democrat because they are voting with an emphasis on justice for life after the womb. We pick and choose based on our own personal histories and priorities; our conscience and how God is guiding us at that time. Regardless, you must only view yourself as a kingdom independent since your primary commitment will be to the kingdom of God over the politics of men.

Joshua learned a great lesson when he stood before the captain of the Lord's army. He learned that God does not pick sides. Nor does God seek to divide. God does not play favorites or seek to exclude. Yet that is what much of politics and elections are about. They are driven by an agenda of division. It seems that more and more of the debates and issues at hand are rooted in an effort to divide different sub-groups throughout the land.

God only votes for Himself and His agenda. And God's agenda is always an agenda of unity under His kingdom rule. Unity brings glory to God. That's the bottom line. And yet so much of what we see Christians participating in regarding their political stance or allegiance involves an atmosphere of vitriol and disunity. The cure for the existing polar divides in our nation rests in God alone. It is only when we return to Him and the prioritization of His will and kingdom agenda on earth that we will regain what we have lost in the areas of unity and harmony in our nation.

No political party ought to ever hold your entire allegiance, because if it veers from God's values and priorities you need to remain committed to God. No politician should supersede God's role in your life. No politician or party should receive the worship you are to give to God alone. Did you notice what Joshua did when he heard the captain of the Lord's army declare who he was and whose side he was on? Joshua didn't argue. He didn't offer his opinion. He didn't point him to a popular talk show or political pundit. No, Joshua fell down on the earth and bowed down before him. When he bowed down on his knees, he was symbolizing his allegiance to God's cause.

We have Christians today who will bow down or take a knee for social causes, but won't bow down before God. It is time for all people who name the name of Jesus Christ to bow before the Almighty God and His kingdom cause. Bowing includes a position of submission. It indicates the intentional yielding to a relationship.

Are you willing to take a knee for God in spite of your political persuasion? Are you willing to take a knee for the King and His kingdom? That's what kingdom voting is all about.

Joshua 6 tells us that when Joshua took a knee before the captain of the Lord's army, he got the answer he needed. He got the strategy he was to deploy in order to win the battle at Jericho. It's in chapter 6, after he submitted to the captain of the Lord's army, that he was given the direction for his supernatural victory.

You and I will get the answers to our nation's issues when we surrender to God Himself. The strategies for our nation's success rest in God. When we come together under Him, we will experience the healing our land so desperately needs. It is only when we can unify under God's overarching kingdom agenda that our collective voices will be heard for good. Politicians often don't have to deal with Christians or our voices because Satan has been so strategic at dividing us. We are broken up into groups of people set against each other rather than working together for God and His glory.

A kingdom voter is someone who understands that they have been given the opportunity and the responsibility to partner with God for the expansion of His rule in society. A kingdom voter understands that God has the ultimate say over all and sits as ruler over all. The closer we align with Him through the voice of our votes, the greater we will experience His power and presence in our land.

Bill Clem was an umpire in the old Negro League. In one of the games he was umpiring, it got to the bottom of the ninth inning. The winning run was on third base. The batter hit a ground ball through the infield, and as the ball was fielded, the runner on third base made his way home to win the game.

It was a dusty day, so as the shortstop threw the ball to the catcher and the catcher went down to tag the runner, the dust flew up at home plate. The dust made it difficult to decide whether the runner was safe or out, and yet the entire game depended on it. As you might imagine, both dugouts emptied.

One group yelled, "Safe!" The other group yelled, "He's out!" As a result, a great conflict erupted on the field. Yet in the midst of the dust and chaos, Bill Clem took off his face mask and threw it down. That's when he shouted, "Everybody shut up! Because it ain't nothing until I call it!" As the dust was flying everywhere, the umpire made the call. And his call was the only call that mattered.

We have a social and political dust storm in our land right now. Democrats are yelling one thing on one side. Republicans are yelling something else on the other side. Dust is flying everywhere. Yet all the while, God is looking down from heaven and shouting, "It ain't nothing until I call it!"

God is the ultimate ruler over all. He has the final say. We get to participate in the process of what He will choose to say through our vote. Our vote is like the runner rounding third base. Will we make it home in time to be called safe? Or will we delay through the ongoing division being stirred up by the enemy of humanity, our spiritual opponent—Satan?

We can make a difference in our nation if we choose to unite under the core values of the kingdom of God. We can help bring healing and prosperity to our land if we come together to seek to implement God's kingdom values through the politicians and policies we support as kingdom citizens and as kingdom independents.

Chapter 11

THE CONSCIENCE OF KINGDOM CITIZENS

When my son Jonathan played for the Buffalo Bills, the team called and asked me to do a chapel service for them. They asked me to speak to the players before their game against Washington. I agreed to the chapel service message, of course, but a few days later I got another call. This time it was from the coach for the opposing team. He had called to also ask me to speak to their team before they faced the Bills.

Now, to be honest, I was hoping the Bills would win because that was the team my son was on. But when the opposing team called me, I knew I needed to speak to them too. After all, God doesn't take sides and both teams needed an injection of His perspective into their situations. So I spoke to both teams, at different times, of course, because I wanted to fulfill my role and responsibility of preaching the Word of God to whomever needs to hear it.

In the chapel services, I was called on to represent heaven and heaven's viewpoint in the midst of a conflict on earth. And even though I held a preference as to who would win in this conflict, I had to remain neutral when presenting heaven's view. I find this illustration meaningful in the day and age in which we live because many of us have a preference when it comes to politics. Many of us lean one way or another. Yet when God calls us to represent Him, whether in the voting booth, on our social platforms, or in general conversations, we need to do so from a position that represents His worldview. We need to step up to the calling of challenging Christians to think heavenly, even though we all hold to earthly preferences.

In spite of the conflict that may take place on the field of political play, we must stand strong to speak and declare the truth in terms of the kingdom of God. We must accept the role and responsibility to partner with God for the advancement of His rule in history as made manifest through the institution of civil government. Regardless of where you may lean, you are to stand with the King. God must remain the dominant influencer of your political belief system, as well as your public declaration.

Yet even with this reality of how we are to function, I do not want to be insensitive to the problem that exists within the body of Christ in that different people have different preferences and alliances. No matter which election is taking place, whether it be local, statewide, or national—we are to guide our thoughts and decisions on the Word of God.

Some people value policy over personality or character. Others value personal character over policy. Some desire expanded government while others push for limited government. Some align more with the support of pro-life regulations while others resonate with justice-based regulations. Whatever the case, one thing remains the same: we are instructed in Scripture to remain true to what we believe. We are to honor our own conscience while trusting God with the ultimate decisions. Proverbs 16:33 puts it like this, "The lot is cast into the lap, but its every decision is from the LORD."

This is a sobering Scripture because all too often it seems that we think we have more of a say than we do. We criticize others and talk like we have more of a say than we do. But even though humanity casts his or her lot, God decides how things will turn out. That's why it is so important to maintain biblical standards in our thoughts, hearts, speech, and participation in politics. Because unless you understand that this is a partnership with God Himself, you can wind up making politics—or even politicians—an idol. You can even wind up using that idol to knock someone else who happens to disagree with you on the head. Politics have become so weaponized in our nation right now, and throughout time, that it is often more effective as a tool for separation than a tool for progress.

You and I must hold fast to the truth that God decides the outcome. When we do, we won't become so easily confused by all the various voices we hear. We won't be so emotionally attached to the polls or even the policies. We won't make politics our new golden calf. Understanding that God controls the outcome through His sovereign ways enables us to rest in the process.

God decides what happens. You may think that people have more power than they do, but God is sovereign. He rules. What we have to keep in mind, though, is that while He rules, He also takes into consideration our choices. He takes into consideration our voices. Your voice and your choice do matter.

Let me explain this more fully by looking at football. In football, you have the sidelines and the goal lines. These are sovereign lines. They are immovable in every game and cannot be negotiated. Yet within those lines, you can call a litany of different plays. You have freedom to move throughout the established lines. What's more, the plays you call or take part in really do matter. It matters to the point of determining whether you move forward or backward on the field.

God has a conditional will. These are the things He decides to do in concert with whether we do what we are supposed to do or not. But He also has a sovereign, unconditional will. These are the things He is going to do regardless of whether you do your part or not. This is why it is critical that each of us does our part. There exist certain things God is only going to do if you and I meet the conditions of obedience.

We can delay or even deny things that God would have been willing to do but were predicated on a condition. For example, if you choose not to vote in an election, you are letting your voice be heard on high. You are letting God know that you do not care enough to participate in the representative process in our land. God will take the votes, or non-votes, of His people into consideration when He sets out to accomplish His sovereign plan.

What we are witnessing today, especially amongst Christians, is the building of walls against one another because of politics and government. We are allowing politics to divide the church. Any agenda of division is straight from hell. When you see a politician or political pundit on television or social media who continually puts forth a narrative that promotes division, you have to question the source. Satan seeks to divide. He is not above using politics to do it, either. That's why it is more important to honor biblical truths than political ideologies. God will hold each of us accountable for how we participated in this game of life. One of the main things He asks of us is stay true to our own belief systems within the boundaries of His Word and sovereign will. We read this in the chapter where we are told to be subject to governing authorities. It's found in Romans 13, where it says,

> Every person is to be in subjection to the governing au-
> thorities. For there is no authority except from God, and
> those which exist are established by God. . . . Therefore it is

necessary to be in subjection, not only because of wrath, but also for conscience' sake. (vv. 1, 5)

The role of your conscience in the decisions you make regarding politics ought to play the primary part. Within the boundaries of God and His Word, you are free to vote or promote that which aligns with your conscience.

Now, everyone's conscience isn't the same, so everyone won't vote the same or promote things the same. But that is the standard we are called to. Which is why it is so dangerous to judge others who do not agree with you. God is viewing their words and actions according to how they align with their conscience, not with yours. Are they honestly reflecting what they believe to be true or are they being manipulated to speak or act in a way that does not internally align? God is not looking at how someone behaves based on someone else's conscience. We are held accountable to the truths of God that resonate within us. This leaves room for differences because everyone's conscience won't be equal when the issues on the table are not perfectly, biblically clear.

What Is Your Conscience

A person's conscience is his or her heart regulator. It is the thing that regulates between right and wrong, good and bad, or up and down. It's the beeper that goes off when somebody comes into your house while it's locked and the alarm system has been turned on. It lets you know that something has gone terribly wrong. It is the light that flashes, begging you to pay attention to avoid the terrible calamity the warning is signaling.

God has built into every human being a conscience, which serves to both govern and guide them. If the conscience is informed properly, it will do its job. But since the heart is deceitfully wicked, an uninformed conscience, or even a corrupted conscience, will drive a person toward wrongdoing (Jer. 17:9). This is why it is critical that everyone's conscience gets the right data in order to make the wisest possible decisions.

But this isn't the case in every person. We are all impacted by a variety of experiences in our lives that either sharpen or dull our consciences. That's why the Bible tells us in Romans 14:1 that we are to accept the person who is weak in faith, and we are not to pass judgment on their opinions. Then the passage goes on to give us practical examples,

> One person has faith that he may eat all things, but he who is weak eats vegetables only. The one who eats is not to regard with contempt the one who does not eat, and the one who does not eat is not to judge the one who eats, for God has accepted him. Who are you to judge the servant of another? To his own master he stands or falls; and he will stand, for the Lord is able to make him stand. One person regards one day above another, another regards every day alike. Each person must be fully convinced in his own mind. He who observes the day, observes it for the Lord, and he who eats, does so for the Lord, for he gives thanks to God; and he who eats not, for the Lord he does not eat, and gives thanks to God. (vv. 2–6)

Paul writes that we are not to judge those who make choices outside of our own, when they do so according to their conscience. When a person's political affiliation causes them to reject, demean, ridicule, curse, or avoid those who differ from them based on their conscience before God, they are violating this passage. We are each on a different plane of advancement and growth. If you were to look at your own life in retrospect, I am sure there are things you believed years ago that you don't now—or vice versa. As we all grow in the Lord, truth and the prioritization of that truth manifests itself differently in our lives.

Everyone in the body of Christ may not feel the same about Democrats or Republicans, or this candidate as opposed to the other candidate, but those differences are not to get in the way of our fellowship together. It is not to get in the way of our service together in advancing God's kingdom on earth. Over the past few years, it has become downright embarrassing to read some of the social media posts and comments filled to the full with vitriol, hatred, and hellishness. And these are posted by Christians to other Christians who happen to disagree with them politically. We have oftentimes become more pagan than the pagans when it comes to publicly voicing our opinions on politics. As followers of Jesus Christ, we ought to talk to each other respectfully, even if we disagree politically. We must recognize the fact that there are good and bad people and policies on both sides of the political divide.

Paul reminds us in this passage that we are not to disregard one another because to do so is an embarrassment to God. We have used our tongues on social media to say the most hideous and hateful things about other Christians just because they are headed in a different direction than us due to a different set of priorities. Some Christians are more "meat-oriented," if we use the "meat/vegetable" illustration in Romans 14. Other Christians are more "vegetable-oriented." That's just the way it is. Yet we are fighting as a body of Christ as if only meat is of God or only vegetables are of God.

What do you think the world must think when they see the hatred in the body of Christ as though one candidate came from heaven and the other candidate came from hell? We act sometimes like one political party is a direct line to God, while the other is Satan himself. I wonder what unbelievers must think about us especially when you can find some of God and some of the devil all the way down the line on both sides. No side is a direct representative from God. Yet we have devolved into a group of people who seem to use the vilest kind of communication or insulting style of memes to align

ourselves publicly with politics. All the while, we are distancing ourselves from Jesus Christ and His principles of love.

It's not wrong to disagree. It's not wrong to vote differently than
another believer. It is wrong, however, to be contemptuous in both.
As verse 3 stated, "The one who eats is not to regard with contempt
the one who does not eat." To regard someone else with contempt because he or she disagrees with you is unChristian. Kingdom-minded
Democrats accept Republicans. Kingdom-minded Republicans
accept Democrats. The reason why each accept the other is because
God accepts both. Thus, when you attack another person in the
family of God because they believe, think, act, or vote differently
than you, you have attacked God. This is no small thing. The division
of our nation down racial, political, class, and even conspiratorial
lines is straight from Satan's playbook.

A person's mouth reflects his or her heart. If your mouth is spew-
ing vitriol at those who disagree with your political affiliation, then
neither your mouth nor your heart is aligned with God. If you have a
cursing mouth, it is because you have a cursing heart. If you have an
evil tongue, it is because you have an evil heart. The way you know how
Christian you are is not by how high you wave your hand in church or
how loud you sing a song. The way you will know is by what comes out
of your mouth. You'll know by what you post or like on social media.
Scripture says, in my Tony Evans's translation, "How dare any of us
regard in contempt someone who disagrees with you?" They are free
to do, say, or believe what they will based on their conscience before
God. It is their conscience God looks at when examining them, not
yours. And you must never seek to bully or force someone to violate a
legitimately held conscience belief.

While we are all growing at different rates, the Bible is to be the
source of our growth and the development of our conscience. If you
disregard a direct command or precept of God that your conscience

knows to be true, then that is sin. Yet within the biblical boundaries of God's Word, God allows freedom.

Some people will vote the way they vote because of the experiences they have had. They've had negative, painful, or even unjust experiences, which have colored their view of life. Others are based on their perception of life, which has colored their priorities. Both are legitimate, but because some families were taught one way and other families were taught another way, every conscience is not the same. People often operate on their upbringing, which causes them to lean in a particular direction. We are not to cut someone down, or disregard them, simply because they do not think like we do. James 4:11 says,

Do not speak against one another, brethren. He who speaks against a brother or judges his brother, speaks against the law and judges the law; but if you judge the law, you are not a doer of the law but a judge of it.

The book of Ephesians puts it like this,

Let no unwholesome word proceed from your mouth, but only such a word as is good for edification according to the need of the moment, so that it will give grace to those who hear. (4:29)

If we were to simply follow this verse in how we speak to those who disagree with us politically, medically, or culturally—we would solve most, if not all, of our nation's social ills. Christians need to come together and set the standard for how we are to function in our land. Christian Democrats, Republicans, Independents, Libertarians—all of us as believers need to reflect God's standard of temperate discourse and respect in what we say and how we act.

God can deal with the differences between us if we learn to focus more on pointing people to God than fueling the flames of division. God sets the standard to which we should all adjust. The problem is, we are so busy pointing out differences that we are failing to raise the weaker consciences up to a higher, biblical standard. We are offending those with weaker consciences rather than inviting them into a healthy discourse to promote greater awareness and growth. We are not to ignore the growth that is needed in the collective conscience at large. We are to look for ways to infuse it with what is needed to promote its development. We are each to live by faith. As Romans 14:22–23 states,

> The faith which you have, have as your own conviction before God. Happy is he who does not condemn himself in what he approves. But he who doubts is condemned if he eats, because his eating is not from faith; and whatever is not from faith is sin.

We are to live according to the truth revealed to us by God, and then do so for the Lord (Rom. 14:8–9). We are to recognize that fellow believers may prioritize certain legitimate biblical principles at a greater level than we do, which may color their political perspective and priorities. If someone had an abortion, for example, they may focus on that issue when they become biblically informed of God's perspective on life. But if another person was affected by injustice or racism, that may be their primary focus. Both are legitimate concerns, but their consciences may provoke them to vote differently.

We are to express Christ in all we do. The problem today is that we do not have enough Christians promoting the faith who have made Jesus Christ their number one priority. How Jesus feels about a political topic, or candidate, or policy, or health mandate, needs to be examined even more than the issues themselves. Jesus is to be Lord in all that we do. He is Lord of everything. Jesus isn't just Lord on Sunday. He isn't just Lord at Bible study. He isn't just Lord when you are doing your devotions. He is also Lord when you post on social media or like other people's posts. He is also Lord when you go into a voting booth or have a conversation with your neighbor about politics, COVID-19, racial issues, or any other pertinent subject of our day.

The problem today is we no longer operate by the lordship of Jesus Christ. Rather, we operate by the lordship of political parties and government entities. I know this to be true because if we truly functioned as a body under the lordship of Jesus Christ, we wouldn't find Christians acting like fools online. We wouldn't experience Christians being divided in the Twittersphere. We wouldn't find Christians embarrassing the kingdom of God in what they say and how they choose to treat others they disagree with.

The Bible tells us, in 1 Peter 3:15, that we are to sanctify the Lord God in our hearts. In other words, we are to get this lordship thing straight. Is Jesus Lord or is your political party lord? That's what it comes down to. Your conscience, given to you by God, should govern how you vote. You are to inform your conscience with the Word of God and then vote or align yourself politically as best you can with it since no political party perfectly aligns with God's kingdom agenda.

Keep in mind, God's definition of civil government is *to maintain a safe, just, righteous, and compassionately responsible environment for freedom to flourish.* With that as our standard, let's no longer be foolish Christians and ignorant saints. Let's not divide the kingdom of God, but instead inform ourselves of what God expects. God expects you to study His Word. He expects you to honor Him in what you say and how you say it. He expects you to be engaged where you can in the political climate of the land. He expects you to advance His kingdom agenda with the time, talents, and treasures He has given to you. Simply put, as kingdom independent voters we are to vote for the persons and policies that best represent and expand the values of the kingdom of God.

These are the things we ought to focus on more fully any time we are headed into a volatile season of politics. We need to emphasize God's standard, and God's standard always begins and ends with love. It is founded on love that reflects the kingdom virtue of kindness in what we say, how we treat others, and what we choose to support.

Chapter 12

THE FUNCTION OF KINGDOM CITIZENS

Christians are now the *visiting team* in our culture. When a professional sports team plays a game at the other team's home field, they are called the visiting team. As the visiting team they go into battle in enemy territory. Not only do they have the opposing team up against them, but the crowds are against them as well.

There existed a time in our nation's history when a Christian worldview informed the culture. We had home-field advantage. And even though the culture had flaws in it, citizens could appeal to a Judeo-Christian frame of reference in order to call the culture back into the proper way of operating. Yet today, we have now become akin to the visiting team in our own nation.

As we've seen throughout this book, the digression of influence in our culture is largely due to the failure of Christians and the church to remain relevant. As a result, we are being booed, marginalized, insulted, rejected, and—more often than not—simply ignored. Yes, God's name does come up from time to time in cultural conversations, but that's about it. We have lost our advantage in the game and, as a result, are tallying up more L's than W's.

But what we must understand and apply to our lives and choices is that even when there exists opposition against you and the crowd is booing you, we are still called to out-perform the opponent. We are still called to win through providing positive influence in a world that needs it badly. We are called to represent the true Ruler and His kingdom rule over all.

I recall a time when I had some serious ant hills on our front lawn. As these ants served their queen, they built mounds on my lawn, turning a once-green lawn into a place of foreign habitation. They were building their own kingdom on my lawn, so I needed to address their presence. If I didn't address it swiftly, they would continue to bring destruction.

What we have today in our nation is the presence of destructive ideologies. We have secularism, humanism, and all forms of idolatry that have invaded our culture and our world. Yet what we need to keep in mind is that God has not called His people to sit on the sidelines of this battle. He has called each of us to step up and get into the game. Now, this goes beyond a certain candidate, or even a group of candidates or political party. This has to do with the role of Christians functioning as kingdom disciples in the culture.

I hope you realize by now that kingdom politics involves so much more than voting. It is a way of life. No matter how you vote or have voted, God is calling you to live as His kingdom follower. He is calling you to something more than being happy or sad about which candidate won or lost. He is calling you to kingdom living and influence.

I love the way Philippians 3:20 declares that "our citizenship is in heaven." We must understand this key truth in order to understand how to live as kingdom citizens in a culture gone astray. Living out of the principles of kingdom politics is rooted in the recognition of where our true allegiance and citizenship reside. You and I are kingdom citizens.

Luke 16:16 affirms this reality in this way,

> The Law and the Prophets were proclaimed until John; since that time the gospel of the kingdom of God has been preached, and everyone is forcing his way into it.

Luke refers to our allegiance as that of the "gospel of the kingdom of God." Thus, as we've seen, a kingdom citizen is *a visible, verbal follower of Jesus Christ who seeks to bring the perspectives of heaven and deposit them into the concerns of the culture.*

LIVING AS ALIENS AND STRANGERS

One of the issues that thwarts our progress in influencing culture for good is that far too many Christians are so earthly-minded that they do nothing toward the heavenly good. They know more about politics than they do about the Lord. They talk more about political parties than they do about the Word of God. They often argue like secularists all while naming the name of Jesus Christ. In fact, if you bring up what God says on a subject, they'll get mad at you even though what you said can be defended by Scripture. This happens more regularly these days because a large segment of the Christian population has become so aligned with the culture that they have lost sight of the truth that their primary citizenship is not here on earth.

I love the way 1 Peter 2:11 puts it when it describes us as "aliens and strangers" in this land. Our citizenship is not first on these shores. Yes, we are residents here, but even so, our allegiance is to another King, another kingdom, and another location. One of the best ways to explain this is to consider how we use passports for travel. When you have a passport, it allows you to enter foreign countries. It does not mean you are now a citizen of the foreign country, but rather you remain a citizen of your homeland that issued your passport. That is, unless you intend to surrender your passport and apply for citizenship in the new land.

Unfortunately, many Christians have surrendered their passports. Some have surrendered their passports to the Democratic party. Others have surrendered their passports to the Republican party. Some of them have surrendered their passports to the cult of athletics, entertainment, or the metaverse. As a result, they no longer think or act as citizens of heaven. They no longer judge or discern as citizens of heaven. Consequently, they no longer influence and impact culture for good as representatives of heaven's kingdom agenda on earth.

When Paul wrote that our citizenship was in heaven in Philippians 3:20, he was writing to the church at Philippi. It's important to note that Philippi was located approximately eight hundred miles from the city of Rome. Paul reminded his readers of their citizenship and emphasized the principle of allegiance despite a lack of physical proximity. While their earthly citizenship was in Rome, over eight hundred miles away, they would still be informed by Roman customs and regulated by Roman laws. They would even be influenced by Roman ways, despite their distance from Rome itself.

Similarly, even though none of us make our physical home in heaven at present, we are to still be informed, regulated, and influenced by heaven's ways. We are a long distance from heaven, but our citizenship is to remain there. You and I are to be dictated by heaven's customs, just like the people of Philippi were dictated to by Caesar.

LIVING WITHOUT PARTY ALLEGIANCES

This is why we are to have no full allegiances here. We can support a side or party or candidate, but we are never to surrender our passport entirely to them. You and I belong to another kingdom and another culture entirely. Just as a thermostat sets the temperature for a thermometer to read, God has called each of us as His kingdom citizens to bring the heat to the culture. We are to set the temperature by establishing norms of kindness, equity, justice, and truth. We are not here just to give a reading of what's in the culture. We are here to impact and affect culture for Christ.

This is not the time to abandon ship. This is a time to lovingly and responsibly take our stand for the lordship of Jesus Christ. This is our time to bring the values of heaven to bear on earth. That's why we are here. God didn't leave us here to sit, sulk, and sour. He didn't leave us here just to go to church on Sunday either. He left us here to penetrate the culture with the customs of heaven. We are to influence our surroundings as both salt and light. Matthew 5:13–16 reminds us of this.

> "You are the salt of the earth; but if the salt has become tasteless, how can it be made salty again? It is no longer good for anything, except to be thrown out and trampled underfoot by men. You are the light of the world. A city set on a hill cannot be hidden; nor does anyone light a lamp and put it under a basket, but on the lampstand, and it gives light to all who are in the house. Let your light shine before men in such a way that they may see your good works, and glorify your Father who is in heaven."

Always remember that you are not the salt of the shaker. Neither are you the light of the bulb. Your role as a kingdom citizen is to infiltrate and influence every sphere of life as a full-time disciple, not as a part-time saint. Everyone ought to know where you stand on issues at hand because you should never be ashamed to speak the truth in love.

You and I are to get our instructions for life from above—from the sweet by-and-by. We are not to be instructed by the nasty here and now. That should no longer be the definitive influence in your life. When people immigrate to this country, for example, they make a declaration that they want to belong here. They declare that they want to be a citizen of the United States of America. They lift their hands, and they pledge allegiance in order to become an American citizen. When they do that, they are releasing their former country's control over them. The old home no longer holds the dominant hand.

Far too many Christians who name the name of Jesus are letting the old way still have sway. That's why when things don't work out like they think they should in the earthly realm, they lose it emotionally. They start fussing, cussing, and complaining. They do this because they have become confused about where their citizenship lies. Colossians 1:13 states it clearly: "For He rescued us from the domain of darkness, and transferred us to the kingdom of His beloved Son."

You are in another kingdom now. You have been transferred to the kingdom of light. This means you are simply a foreigner here. This is not your permanent location. America is a temporary passport location. You are no longer to act like this culture sets your definitions anymore. You are to take your stand. If someone asks you if you are a Democrat or a Republican, you should respond with, "What issue are you talking about?" Because neither the Democratic party or the Republican party completely aligns with God's Word. It depends on the issue at hand. That means a person could be Democrat on some issues and Republican on others. But, regardless, they should be for the kingdom all the time. That's why I like to refer to myself as a *kingdom independent*. This reflects my belief that I am to represent heaven on the issues at hand.

When we look at the context for Paul's statement on heavenly citizenship, we can see what prompts him to say what he did. The verse leading up to it gives a clear view. We read, "Whose end is destruction, whose god is their appetite, and whose glory is in their shame, who set their minds on earthly things." Paul wanted to encourage them not to think in earthly terms. To stop thinking like a secularist. To stop

THE FUNCTION OF KINGDOM CITIZENS

thinking in terms of the old home, or the old way, or the old country. The Bible calls this kind of thinking "worldliness." It's also sometimes referred to as "human wisdom," when a person has adopted a way of thinking that is incongruent with a kingdom mindset.

Paul wrote what he did in order to call each of us away from the issue of having divided thoughts. He wanted to remind us to set our minds on God and His heavenly kingdom agenda. When we do that, we won't vacillate between two opinions. We won't become irrelevant to the cultural issues at hand. We will bring sense, order, and answers to a society in need of all three.

LIVING WITH A KINGDOM PERSPECTIVE

As we conclude our time together, I want to ask you to consider if you regularly bring heaven's view into the discussion on politics. Do you bring a kingdom perspective to the discussions on platforms? Or do you revert to earthly thoughts that are anti-God and anti-truth? Unfortunately, we have become a platform of parties that won't open the Bible anymore. We won't ask anyone to explain what Scripture has to say. And we are suffering the results of this spiritual exclusion from politics.

Government belongs to God. He's got something to say on every issue. James 3 calls God's thoughts wisdom from above, but in this passage he also points out that there is

We have become a platform of parties that won't open the Bible anymore.

"earthly wisdom" too. It is wisdom that comes from demons. We read,

> Who among you is wise and understanding? Let him show by his good behavior his deeds in the gentleness of wisdom. But if you have bitter jealousy and selfish ambition in your heart,

do not be arrogant and so lie against the truth. This wisdom is not that which comes down from above, but is earthly, natural, demonic. For where jealousy and selfish ambition exist, there is disorder and every evil thing. But the wisdom from above is first pure, then peaceable, gentle, reasonable, full of mercy and good fruits, unwavering, without hypocrisy. And the seed whose fruit is righteousness is sown in peace by those who make peace. (James 3:13–18)

James lets us know in this passage that so-called "earthly wisdom" is demonic thought. If what you think, say, or hear disagrees with what God says on the subject, you have just taken sides with demons. You have become demonized. Because of this, we have a lot of demonized Christians walking around talking about politics, policies, and priorities emphasizing the world's standards instead of God's. In essence, they have switched teams altogether and joined the cohort of earthlings.

Jesus made it clear where He was from and what He stood for. In John 18, we read about a critical conversation between Him and Pilate shortly before His crucifixion. Jesus makes it known that the kingdom He represents and leads is not of earth. The conversation goes as follows,

Therefore Pilate entered again into the Praetorium, and summoned Jesus and said to Him, "Are You the King of the Jews?" Jesus answered, "Are you saying this on your own initiative, or did others tell you about Me?" Pilate answered, "I am not a Jew, am I? Your own nation and the chief priests delivered You to me; what have You done?" Jesus answered, "My kingdom is not of this world. If My kingdom were of this world, then My servants would be fighting so that I would not be handed over to the Jews; but as it is, My kingdom is not of this realm." Therefore Pilate said to Him, "So You are a king?"

Jesus answered, "You say correctly that I am a king. For this I have been born, and for this I have come into the world, to testify to the truth. Everyone who is of the truth hears My voice." (vv. 33–38)

Jesus testifies to the truth. He reveals the truth. He lets us know as we live in an atmosphere of deception what is up and what is down, what is right and what is wrong. The reason so many of us are not hearing answers to our prayers is because we have turned a deaf ear to truth. We don't want the truth anymore. That's why Jesus makes it known that the kingdom He runs is not of this world. Rather, it has come into this world to influence and impact it.

That's why one of the first questions you should ask about anything and everything when you choose to live as a kingdom citizen is, What does God say on the matter? Truth matters. And there is only one Source of truth in existence. When people are caught in a traffic jam, they will often turn on a news app or news station on the radio to hear from a different perspective. They want to hear from the person in the helicopter who can see more clearly than they can. Or they want to see what the satellite images show so they can know whether or not to divert from their intended direction or to simply wait it out.

Helicopter traffic reporters and satellite images give you a different view than what you normally can see behind the wheel. It will give you a view from on high. That new view then informs your thoughts and affects your decisions so that you can still get to where you need to go, but in the least cumbersome way. The reason you get more information is because more can be seen from up high. Similarly, God sees more than you and I can see down here. We need His insight and perspective from on high in order to make the right decisions down here. If we decide to make our decisions based only on what we can see in front of us, similar to a driver stuck in traffic, we won't know the best possible path to take. God offers us a vantage point that will help us navigate not only the decisions we have to make but also the emotions, which often arise due to issues we face.

It's only when we commit to His ways that we will find the best path forward in life. What would you think of a driver who was shown the quickest path on his traffic app but decided to sit in the mess of cars anyhow and continue to complain? You would probably scratch your head like I would and wonder why did he bother to look at his traffic app in the first place. The problem today is that we have way too many Christians living with this double standard. They will glance at God's Word only to choose to stay stuck in the mess, mire, and muck of earth's issues and complain. Thus, while God gives the way out to experience peace in emotions and a path forward, James reminds us that when we live according to this double standard, we can expect that even our prayers will go unanswered. We read about this in James 1:5–8,

> But if any of you lacks wisdom, let him ask of God, who gives to all generously and without reproach, and it will be given to him. But he must ask in faith without any doubting, for the one who doubts is like the surf of the sea, driven and tossed by the wind. For that man ought not to expect that he will receive anything from the Lord, being a double-minded man, unstable in all his ways.

We've got AM/FM Christians who keep switching channels on God only to blame Him when things continue to be fuzzy in their lives. They may tune into the HBS (Heavenly Broadcast System) on Sunday only to tune into the SBN (Secular Broadcast Network) the rest of the week. That's part-time Christianity. God is calling us to a higher standard. Until we get a true radicalization among God's followers who choose to live according to His standard and worldview, we will not see the supernatural enter into the natural to bring order to a chaotic environment. We have turned to looking at mere men instead of God Himself.

I love Gideon's response in Judges 8:22–23 when the people called on him to lead them. Gideon made it clear who was in charge, and who should remain in charge. We read,

> Then the men of Israel said to Gideon, "Rule over us, both you and your son, also your son's son, for you have delivered us from the hand of Midian." But Gideon said to them, "I will not rule over you, nor shall my son rule over you; the Lord shall rule over you."

The people expressed their desire for Gideon to lead them as a political ruler. But Gideon knew where that would ultimately lead. The mess in our society today is an example of what happens when people look to people rather than to God Himself. We are continuing to experience one problem after another because the solutions being presented are like trying to put a Band-Aid on a gaping wound. If we want real solutions to the real problems that plague us as a nation and a land, we've got to bring God back into the equation. We've got to appeal to His divine standard as the standard by which we should measure our decisions as a nation. We've got to realize that although it seems that the president or Congress may be in charge, there is only One who is truly in charge of all. We read who this is in Matthew 28:18, "And Jesus came up and spoke to them, saying, 'All authority has been given to Me in heaven and on earth.'"

Jesus is the "head" of all things (Eph. 1:22–23). And He expresses His leadership and rule through His church. God is going to decide what He does for our country, or for any country, based on what the church does in response to His Word. If we don't fix the church house, we can forget about the White House. If we don't address the church house, we can forget about the house of Congress.

God has always worked through the church in order to express His rule to the principalities, powers, and authorities in culture.

We are to be in the world, but not of the world. Our loyalty is not here. Until we satisfy the issue of the lordship of Jesus Christ and our allegiance to Him and His rule, we will continue to crumble as a nation. When we follow Jesus as Lord, we actively advance His kingdom and values through all we do and say. This isn't done violently or forcibly, but neither is it done passively. We are to be consistent in the promotion of kingdom values throughout the land. We are to do it with love, but we are still to do it. Love doesn't mean we surrender our passports and agree with everyone on everything. Love means we promote truth, righteousness, and justice in every opportunity we can while challenging our political leaders to do the same.

A very common wartime strategy is known as the *fifth column*. When a country deploys a fifth-columnist approach to war, they seek to infiltrate the culture in order to impact the culture in the way they want. They send people into the opposing country to assimilate and become doctors, educators, politicians, businesspeople, judges, and more. In this way, they can destroy the opposing country from within. It turns into a strategy of sabotage. Sometimes this sabotage takes place prior to a larger invasion. But other times, it is enough on its own to deflate a nation of its resources in order for it to become vulnerable enough for a quick and easy defeat.

Jesus has sent you and me into this world prior to His return in order to set up His kingdom agenda in all areas of life, including the political realm. Remember, Jesus is always on the ballot. We are to be His fifth columnists sent in to set things up for the big invasion of His earthly kingdom called His Millennial Reign. We are to influence culture in every capacity we can so that the values of the kingdom of God become the dominant values in the land. We are to take our stand in society so that we set up the return of the one, true King. That's what living as a kingdom citizen means. It means that we emphasize and promote God's values in a world that seeks to leave Him out.

As a kingdom citizen, your allegiance is to God and your vote or voice must be clear. There is no undecided voter when it comes to living as a Christian. Depending on what the issue is, you need to take your stand for Him.

One of the reasons so many Jews lost their lives to Hitler in the Holocaust was because the church was silent. Hitler was an evil man leading an evil empire whose goal it was to exterminate an entire group of people. He told the pastors in his land that they could talk about anything they wanted, just not politics. If they conducted their services without discussing politics, he would leave them alone. Those who went against his order of silence paid the price. Dietrich Bonhoeffer was one of them.

Yet the majority looked the other way. In fact, stories are told of trains full of Jewish people being sent off to concentration camps having to pass by churches full of people. When the trains would get closer to the churches, the people inside would simply sing louder so as to not hear the moans and groans of those being taken away to their death. Unfortunately today, too many Christians in churches are singing louder while lives are going to hell. Too many Christians are turning up the sports channels or political pundits or entertainment so that they can't hear the moans and groans of those Satan is carting off to destruction. Too many pastors are preaching safe sermons rather than sermons that truly make an impact in our culture. As a result, our culture continues its steady decline into a state of destruction.

Kingdom citizens must do better than this. God's goal in history is that all issues are to be brought under the lordship of Jesus Christ (Eph. 1:10, 22–23; 1 Cor. 15:28). With an allegiance to Christ, we must publicly declare where God stands on the issues our country faces. We must be more than a churchgoer—we must also engage the culture. We must bring a Christian influence into every place we go, whether it's business, education, work, or in our relationships. We need to show up at the PTA meetings or become more involved in the education of our children. We need to attend the city council meetings and hear about what is happening or planned for our local communities. If there are unjust practices taking place, we need to bring it up to those who may not know but who could join in to make a difference for good.

The trajectory of our nation can be reversed. Kingdom citizens can influence police-community relations, policies, health care reform, and more. We do it through standing up as citizens of heaven while drawing down God's viewpoint into earth's decisions. In all we do, we need to represent God first.

What our world is in desperate need of are kingdom disciples. These are committed Christians who view and live all of life in submission to the lordship of Jesus Christ. They have transformed lives that seek to replicate God's kingdom values in the lives of others as well as in the societal structures that affect them. It is through these disciples that God exercises His authority from heaven into history.

Doctors are not to be just doctors, but they are to be God's representatives in the medical field so the medical field sees what God looks like when God helps hurting people. Lawyers are not just lawyers. They are God's representatives in the Bar Association so that people get to see what God looks like when He enacts or defends justice. Teachers are not just teachers. They are God's representatives in the educational field so the educational field sees what God looks like when God values learning and education. Homemakers are not just homemakers. They are God's representatives in the home to ensure that their home reflects the values and character of God. Men are to have their masculinity defined by God, not the culture. Women are to have their femininity defined by God, not the culture. Living in this way leads to the opportunity to create kingdom people who are citizens of heaven and not mimics of the culture.

We must understand that there is no salvation in politics. There is no savior who is going to show up in the political realm. If God is not postured properly in the hearts and minds of a nation's citizens, it doesn't matter who is elected to lead. The more secular a country becomes, the less of God that country will see. The less of God that is seen, the more chaos will ensue. Thus, the church better shake itself up, wake up, and get up so that we can see what God can do when people commit their lives to Him as citizens of His kingdom, honoring Him as King.

One day a man was headed to a shoe shop to get his shoe fixed, but he arrived just a minute too late. The shop closed at 5 p.m. But even though the shop was closed, he could see the shop owner on the inside, so he decided to knock on the door. The shoe man called out, "I'm closed."

The man replied, "Please, I didn't mean to be late. I need to get my shoes dropped off."

The proprietor decided to open the door and let him in. While he was in dropping off his shoes to be fixed, he mentioned that he didn't see any cars in the parking lot and wondered how the proprietor had planned to get home. "I'm already home," the owner replied.

Seeing the confusion on the face of the customer, he continued, "See those stairs over there? They go upstairs. I live upstairs. I just work down here."

If you are going to be a kingdom citizen proficient in the subject of kingdom politics, making an impact for the kingdom in our culture, you have to remember where you live. In order to bring the concerns of heaven and execute them into the chaos of the culture, you must do so as a visible, verbal follower of Jesus Christ. You must do so in the awareness that you live up there. Your citizenship is in heaven. You just work down here.

Conclusion

A KINGDOM STRATEGY FOR COMMUNITY TRANSFORMATION

Since the church is the primary manifestation of the kingdom and is the primary means by which God is extending His kingdom rule in this world, local churches must consider what we can do together to bring about positive outcomes in society and in politics. We must be willing to work together across racial, denominational, and class lines. Churches should cooperate in a comprehensive program that connects both the spiritual and social. Churches must work together to extend their influence beyond their individual walls in order to impact the broader communities that they serve.

The crying need today is for churches to become discipleship training centers for developing their members to become kingdom disciples who learn to progressively bring all of life under the lordship of Jesus Christ (Matt. 28:18–20). The church is God's authorized kingdom agency that has been given divine authority (i.e., keys of the kingdom) to exercise kingdom authority on God's behalf in history (Matt. 16:18–19).

As such, and as we have seen earlier, we are to function as salt and light in society (Matt. 5:13–16) in order to bring divine influence into our cultural reality. We must seek to offer, encourage, and enact practical ways for individuals and churches to repair the fissures of our racial divide. For far too long, believers have looked to political, economic, social, and education-based agendas to address the decay now engulfing us. But spiritual success in a spiritual war depends entirely upon spiritual solutions.

The kingdom-minded church must accept the responsibility and challenge of leading the way in reversing our political divides since we, to a large degree, are responsible in helping to keep it enflamed.

God has given us a three-pronged Kingdom Strategy for Community Transformation for churches to consider adopting and implementing across political lines in every community. I call this "A Kingdom Strategy for Community Transformation: A 3-Point Plan for Positive Cultural Impact." You can download this plan for free by visiting our ministry website (tonyevans.org). It is easily accessible on our ministry homepage.

The decay of our culture is, at its core, a spiritual issue. That is why we believe when the church decides to operate in unity on a kingdom-based agenda that we will usher in true and lasting hope for our land. Churches must come together across political and cultural lines and work toward positive impact. We must heed the clarion call, from heaven into history and from eternity into time, for Christians to live fully as kingdom disciples.

Unless kingdom-minded influencers enter the discussion and assume leadership for promoting the pillars of justice and righteousness in society in order to resolve the existing crisis, we will be hopelessly deadlocked in a sea of relativity regarding all issues. This will result in more questions rather than permanent answers. God is not going to bless a country or a culture that comes up with its own rules and asks Him to bless it. God expects kingdom-minded churches to lead the way.

This is a defining moment for us as churches and citizens to decide whether we want to be one nation under God or a divided nation apart from God. If we don't answer that question correctly, and if we don't answer it quickly, we won't be much of a nation at all (2 Chron. 15:3–6; Ps. 33:12).

I have proposed this 3-Point Plan for positive cultural impact through the church. This plan involves the following three foundational components:

1. Assemble: Unified Sacred Gathering

Kingdom-minded pastors or leaders develop a community-wide pastors' fellowship that meets regularly and hosts an annual solemn assembly (Isa. 58:1–12; Eph. 2:11–22).

2. Address: Unified Compassionate Voice

Kingdom-minded pastors or leaders actively develop disciples who speak out with a unified message, offering biblical truths and solutions on contemporary cultural issues (John 17:13–23; Matt. 28:16–20).

3. Act: Unified Social Impact

Kingdom-minded pastors or leaders collectively mobilize their churches or organizations to carry out a visible presence of ongoing good works, improving the well-being of underserved communities (Jer. 29:5–7; Matt. 5:13–16).

1. Assemble: Unified Sacred Gathering

Have you ever noticed how special interest groups in our country carry far more weight in influencing our policies and opinions, even though their numbers are but a small fraction of the number of believers in America? They carry so much weight and influence because they unite.

We may have the numbers in our favor as an overall body of believers, but we have rarely, if ever, truly united over anything. It is time to set our preferences and egos aside and go before the Lord as one body. The problem is not merely our waiting on God to involve Himself in our country's demise, but it is also that God is waiting on us to call on Him collectively, and according to His prescribed manner. I have compiled the following action items (aimed at spiritual leaders) to help us achieve this first point of the 3-Point Plan:

- Start or join a racially and denominationally diverse fellowship of kingdom-minded pastors in your local area.
- Meet regularly with kingdom-minded pastors to strengthen relationships, provide mutual encouragement, and to meet the needs of one another.
- Worship together and seek God in prayer.
- Use social and digital media to facilitate communication with your fellow spiritual leaders.
- Train and develop lay leaders who can provide practical assistance and support for meeting your goals.
- Plan and host a local solemn assembly at least once a year, gathering congregations together to seek God on behalf of their community and the nation. Share your pulpit on occasion with like-minded pastors across racial, class, and denominational divides.

2. Address: Unified Compassionate Voice

The second point in the 3-Point Plan is to address the issues at hand through a unified, compassionate voice. If we could agree to speak in unison on our ideologies and theologies of agreement—rather than spend all our time arguing the portions of disagreement—we would do better at calming the anger and hostilities in our churches and land. In so doing, we could offer several productive and impactful options for restoration and biblically based equity.

A number of special interest groups have been successful in influencing culture because they have managed to unify their collective voice both in the media and entertainment, even though they are small in number. It is time to set our platforms and personal agendas aside when it comes to the matters of national importance so that we can effectively speak into and address the concerns of our day. Here are some steps our spiritual leaders can take in order to do this:

- Seek common ground and shared goals that foster biblical solutions to contemporary issues needing to be addressed, rather than get hung up on the areas of disagreement. Show grace.
- Hold discussion groups and prayer sessions to explore the biblical answers to cultural issues.
- Read and discuss relevant books and videos together to form a basis for common understanding.
- Commit to serving together to work for cultural transformation and biblical values.
- Host community forums to address relevant social issues.
- Collectively meet with civic leaders for relationship building to address issues related to justice and righteousness, and in an effort to influence needed policy reforms.
- Reestablish the biblical importance, permanence, and centrality of marriage and the family as the foundation for a stable and productive society.
- Equip and deploy church members to be kingdom

disciples who have transformed lives that visibly transfer the values of the kingdom of God into the societal spheres of politics, education, law, medicine, business, entertainment, etc.

- Utilize the pulpit, platforms, and other ministry opportunities to give an equal emphasis to the issue of justice as is done with righteousness.

3. Act: Unified Social Impact

The third point of the 3-Point Plan is to act together to bring about unified social impact. We will make a bigger impact when we intentionally align our actions with each other in order to produce greater momentum. Here are some action items that can assist ministry and lay leaders:

- Pray for wisdom and guidance as to how you can partner in good works together.
- Work together toward meeting the needs of the local homeless population.
- Implement the "Kindness in the Culture" initiative by distributing "Acts of Kindness" cards to your church members or community group. Encourage them to perform a random "act of kindness" for anyone in need, then give them a card with the information of their local church on it, or other information, and ask them if they can pray for them or present the gospel.
- Coordinate a collective voice in petitions, letter writing, phone calls, and other ways to influence political leadership to bring about righteous and just policy and legislative reforms.
- Create an atmosphere where congregants are challenged

to pursue relationships promoting racial reconciliation while simultaneously working toward biblical justice.

- Seek ways to collectively address shortages of food, housing, and other basic needs of underserved families in your community.
- Equip and/or shape the mindset of church members regarding a kingdom perspective as they engage with the culture.
- Build relationships with local law enforcement to foster a stronger relationship and serve as a bridge between the police and the community.
- Construct a network for business leaders who want to assist in creating employment opportunities and economic development for underserved communities.
- Identify key service agencies in your community that you can collectively support in order to facilitate a beneficial kingdom impact.

When we come together to **Assemble, Address**, and **Act** on behalf of God's kingdom in society at large, we will bring about a greater impact as a whole. The scope of our unity will determine the scope of our impact.

THE URBAN ALTERNATIVE

The Urban Alternative (TUA) equips, empowers, and unites Christians to impact *individuals, families, churches,* and *communities* through a thoroughly kingdom agenda worldview. In teaching truth, we seek to transform lives.

The core cause of the problems we face in our personal lives, homes, churches, and societies is a spiritual one; therefore, the only way to address it is spiritually. We've tried a political, social, economic, and even a religious agenda.

It's time for a **kingdom agenda**.

The kingdom agenda can be defined as the visible manifestation of the comprehensive rule of God over every area of life.

The unifying central theme throughout the Bible is the glory of God and the advancement of His kingdom. The conjoining thread from Genesis to Revelation—from beginning to end—is focused on one thing: God's glory through advancing God's kingdom.

When you do not recognize that theme, the Bible becomes disconnected stories that are great for inspiration but seem to be unrelated in purpose and direction. Understanding the role of the kingdom in Scripture increases the relevancy of this several thousand-year-old text to your day-to-day living, because the kingdom is not only then, it is now.

The absence of the kingdom's influence in our personal lives, family lives, churches, and communities has led to a deterioration in our world of immense proportions:

- People live segmented, compartmentalized lives because they lack God's kingdom worldview.
- Families disintegrate because they exist for their own satisfaction rather than for the kingdom.
- Churches are limited in the scope of their impact because they fail to comprehend that the goal of the church is not the church itself, but the kingdom.
- Communities have nowhere to turn to find real solutions for real people who have real problems because the church has become divided, ingrown, and unable to transform the cultural and political landscape in any relevant way.

The kingdom agenda offers us a way to see and live life with a solid hope by optimizing the solutions of heaven. When God is no longer the final and authoritative standard under which all else falls, order and hope leave with Him. But the reverse of that is true as well: as long as you have God, you have hope. If God is still in the picture, and as long as His agenda is still on the table, it's not over.

Even if relationships collapse, God will sustain you. Even if finances dwindle, God will keep you. Even if dreams die, God will revive you. As long as God and His rule are still the overarching standard in your life, family, church, and community, there is always hope.

Our world needs the King's agenda. Our churches need the King's agenda. Our families need the King's agenda.

We've put together a three-part plan to direct us to heal the divisions and strive for unity as we move toward the goal of truly being one nation under God. This three-part plan calls us to assemble with others in unity, address the issues that divide us, and to act together for social impact. Following this plan, we will see individuals, families, churches, and communities transformed as we follow God's kingdom agenda in every area of our lives. You can request this plan by emailing info@tonyevans.org, or by going online to tonyevans.org.

In many major cities, there is a loop that drivers can take when they want to get somewhere on the other side of the city but don't necessarily want to head straight through downtown. This loop will take you close enough to the city so that you can see its towering buildings and skyline, but not close enough to actually experience it.

This is precisely what we, as a culture, have done with God. We have put Him on the "loop" of our personal, family, church, and community lives. He's close enough to be at hand should we need Him in an emergency, but far enough away that He can't be the center of who we are.

We want God on the "loop," not the King of the Bible who comes downtown into the very heart of our ways. Leaving God on the "loop" brings about dire consequences as we have seen in our own lives and with others. But when we make God and His rule the centerpiece of all we think, do, or say, it is then that we will experience Him in the way He longs for us to.

He wants us to be kingdom people with kingdom minds set on fulfilling His kingdom's purposes. He wants us to pray, as Jesus did,

"Not my will, but Thy will be done." Because His is the kingdom, the power, and the glory.

There is only one God, and we are not Him. As King and Creator, God calls the shots. It is only when we align ourselves under His comprehensive hand that we will access His full power and authority in all spheres of life: personal, familial, ecclesiastical, and governmental.

As we learn how to govern ourselves under God, we then transform the institutions of family, church, and society using a biblically based kingdom worldview.

Under Him, we touch heaven and change earth.

To achieve our goal, we use a variety of strategies, approaches, and resources for reaching and equipping as many people as possible.

BROADCAST MEDIA

Millions of individuals experience *The Alternative with Dr. Tony Evans* through the daily radio broadcast playing on nearly **1,400 radio outlets** and in over **130 countries**. The broadcast can also be seen on several television networks and is available online at TonyEvans.org. You can also listen or view the daily broadcast by downloading the Tony Evans app for free in the App store. Over thirty million message downloads/streams occur each year.

LEADERSHIP TRAINING

The Tony Evans Training Center (TETC) facilitates a comprehensive discipleship platform, which provides an educational program that embodies the ministry philosophy of Dr. Tony Evans as expressed through the kingdom agenda. The training courses focus on leadership development and discipleship in the following five tracks:

- Bible and Theology
- Personal Growth
- Family and Relationships
- Church Health and Leadership Development
- Society and Community Impact Strategies

The TETC program includes courses for both local and online students. Furthermore, TETC programming includes course work for non-student attendees. Pastors, Christian leaders, and Christian laity, both local and at a distance, can seek out The Kingdom Agenda Certificate for personal, spiritual, and professional development. For more information, visit: TonyEvansTraining.org

The Kingdom Agenda Pastors (KAP) provides a *viable network* for *like-minded pastors* who embrace the kingdom agenda philosophy. Pastors have the opportunity to go deeper with Dr. Tony Evans as they are given greater biblical knowledge, practical applications, and resources to impact individuals, families, churches, and communities. KAP welcomes *senior and associate pastors* of all churches. KAP also offers an annual Summit held each year in Dallas with intensive seminars, workshops, and resources. For more information, visit: KAFellowship.org.

Pastors' Wives Ministry, founded by Dr. Lois Evans, provides *counsel, encouragement,* and *spiritual resources* for pastors' wives as they serve with their husbands in the ministry. A primary focus of the ministry is the KAP Summit offers senior pastors' wives a safe place to *reflect, renew,* and *relax,* along with training in personal development, spiritual growth, and care for their emotional and physical well-being. For more information, visit: LoisEvans.org

KINGDOM COMMUNITY IMPACT

The outreach programs of The Urban Alternative seek to provide positive impact to individuals, churches, families, and communities through a variety of ministries. We see these efforts as necessary to our calling as a ministry and essential to the communities we serve. With training on how to initiate and maintain programs to adopt schools, or provide homeless services, or partner toward unity and justice with the local police precincts, which creates a connection between the police and our community, we, as a ministry, live out God's kingdom agenda according to our *Kingdom Strategy for Community Transformation*.

The Kingdom Strategy for Community Transformation is a three-part plan that equips churches to have a positive impact on their communities for the kingdom of God. It also provides numerous practical suggestions for how this three-part plan can be implemented in your community, and it serves as a blueprint for unifying churches around the common goal of creating a better world for all of us. For more information, visit: TonyEvans.org and click on the link to access the 3-Point Plan.

National Church Adopt-a-School Initiative (NCAASI) prepares churches across the country to impact communities by using *public schools as the primary vehicle for effecting positive social change* in urban youth and families. Leaders of churches, school districts, faith-based organizations and other nonprofit organizations are equipped with the knowledge and tools to *forge partnerships* and build *strong social service delivery systems*. This training is based on the comprehensive church-based community impact strategy conducted by Oak Cliff Bible Fellowship. It addresses such areas as economic development, education, housing, health revitalization, family renewal, and racial reconciliation. We assist churches in tailoring the model to meet specific needs of their communities while simultaneously addressing the spiritual and moral frame of reference. Training events are held annually in the Dallas area at Oak Cliff Bible Fellowship. For more information, visit: ChurchAdoptASchool.org.

Athlete's Impact (AI) exists as an outreach both into and through the sports arena. Coaches can be the most influential factor in young people's lives, even ahead of their parents. With the growing rise of fatherlessness in our culture, more young people are looking to their coaches for guidance, character development, practical needs, and hope. After coaches on the influencer scale fall athletes. Athletes (whether professional or amateur) influence younger athletes and kids within their spheres of impact. Knowing this, we have made it our aim to equip and train coaches and athletes on how to live out and utilize their God-given roles for the benefit of the kingdom. We aim to do this through our iCoach App as well as resources such as *The Playbook: A Life Strategy Guide for Athletes*. For more information, visit: ICoachApp.org.

Tony Evans Films ushers in positive life change through compelling video shorts, animation, and feature-length films. We seek to build kingdom disciples through the power of story. We use a variety of platforms for viewer consumption and have over one hundred million digital views. We also merge video shorts and film with relevant Bible study materials to bring people to the saving knowledge of Jesus Christ and to strengthen the body of Christ worldwide. *Tony Evans Films* released the first feature-length film, *Kingdom Men Rising*, in April 2019 in over eight hundred theaters nationwide, in partnership with Lifeway Films. The second release, *Journey with Jesus*, is in partnership with RightNow Media.

RESOURCE DEVELOPMENT

We are fostering lifelong learning partnerships with the people we serve by providing a variety of published materials. Dr. Evans has published more than 125 unique titles based on over fifty years of preaching, whether that is in booklet, book, or Bible study format. He also holds the honor of writing and publishing the first full-Bible commentary and study Bible by an African American, released in 2019. This Bible sits in permanent display as a historic release, in The Museum of the Bible in Washington, D.C.

For more information, and a complimentary copy of Dr. Evans's devotional newsletter, call (800) 800–3222 *or* write TUA at P.O. Box 4000, Dallas TX 75208, *or* visit us online.

www.tonyevans.org

SCRIPTURE INDEX

OLD TESTAMENT

| 6:1 | 162 | 2:2 | 39, 117 |

Galatians
| 1:15–16 | 80 |
| 5:13 | 56 |

Titus
| 2:1, 6 | 147 |

Ephesians
1:10	195
1:11	16
1:22–23	112, 193, 195
2:11–22	201
2:21–22	112
3:10	116
4:29	179
5:22–24	147
6:4	101

Hebrews
11:31	152
13:8	10
13:17	147, 148

James
1:5–8	192
3:9	83
3:13–18	189–90
4:11	179
4:12	36, 59, 109
5:1–6	132

Philippians
| 2:4 | 128 |
| 3:20 | 184, 186 |

1 Peter
2:11	185
2:13	147
2:13–14	69, 157
2:17	158
3:15	181

Colossians
| 1:13 | 188 |
| 1:16–17 | 10 |

2 Thessalonians
| 3:10 | 130 |

Revelation
1:5	10
7:9	27
13:15–18	20
13:16–17	138
19:6	17
19:16	10

1 Timothy
1:8–10	35
2:1–2	157
2:1–4	114–15

RECONCILIATION, THE KINGDOM, AND HOW WE ARE STRONGER TOGETHER

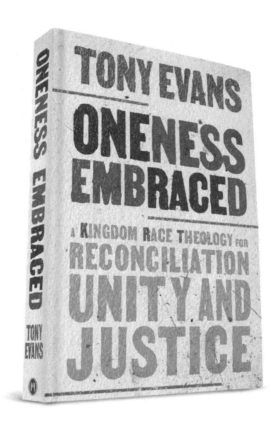

MOODY
Publishers®

From the Word to Life®

In this legacy message, Tony Evans seeks to overcome the racial divide and promote a biblical understanding of the kingdom foundation of oneness by detailing why we don't have it, what we need to do to get it, and what it will look like when we live it. To better glorify God and help heal the persistent racial divide, all church members would do well to read and learn from *Oneness Embraced*.

978-0-8024-2472-3 | also available as an eBook